MW00345616

IDEX
California Exam
SECRETS

Study Guide
Your Key to Exam Success

IDEX Test Review for the
California Interior Design Examination

Dear Future Exam Success Story:

Congratulations on your purchase of our study guide. Our goal in writing our study guide was to cover the content on the test, as well as provide insight into typical test taking mistakes and how to overcome them.

Standardized tests are a key component of being successful, which only increases the importance of doing well in the high-pressure high-stakes environment of test day. How well you do on this test will have a significant impact on your future, and we have the research and practical advice to help you execute on test day.

The product you're reading now is designed to exploit weaknesses in the test itself, and help you avoid the most common errors test takers frequently make.

How to use this study guide

We don't want to waste your time. Our study guide is fast-paced and fluff-free. We suggest going through it a number of times, as repetition is an important part of learning new information and concepts.

First, read through the study guide completely to get a feel for the content and organization. Read the general success strategies first, and then proceed to the content sections. Each tip has been carefully selected for its effectiveness.

Second, read through the study guide again, and take notes in the margins and highlight those sections where you may have a particular weakness.

Finally, bring the manual with you on test day and study it before the exam begins.

Your success is our success

We would be delighted to hear about your success. Send us an email and tell us your story. Thanks for your business and we wish you continued success.

Sincerely,

Mometrix Test Preparation Team

Need more help? Check out our flashcards at: http://MometrixFlashcards.com/IDEX

Copyright © 2017 by Mometrix Media LLC. All rights reserved.
Written and edited by the Mometrix Exam Secrets Test Prep Team
Printed in the United States of America

TABLE OF CONTENTS

Top 20 Test Taking Tips

1. Carefully follow all the test registration procedures
2. Know the test directions, duration, topics, question types, how many questions
3. Setup a flexible study schedule at least 3-4 weeks before test day
4. Study during the time of day you are most alert, relaxed, and stress free
5. Maximize your learning style; visual learner use visual study aids, auditory learner use auditory study aids
6. Focus on your weakest knowledge base
7. Find a study partner to review with and help clarify questions
8. Practice, practice, practice
9. Get a good night's sleep; don't try to cram the night before the test
10. Eat a well balanced meal
11. Know the exact physical location of the testing site; drive the route to the site prior to test day
12. Bring a set of ear plugs; the testing center could be noisy
13. Wear comfortable, loose fitting, layered clothing to the testing center; prepare for it to be either cold or hot during the test
14. Bring at least 2 current forms of ID to the testing center
15. Arrive to the test early; be prepared to wait and be patient
16. Eliminate the obviously wrong answer choices, then guess the first remaining choice
17. Pace yourself; don't rush, but keep working and move on if you get stuck
18. Maintain a positive attitude even if the test is going poorly
19. Keep your first answer unless you are positive it is wrong
20. Check your work, don't make a careless mistake

Copyright © Mometrix Media. You have been licensed one copy of this document for personal use only. Any other reproduction or redistribution is strictly prohibited. All rights reserved.

Administration

Obtaining a building permit

In the state of California, the first step to obtaining a building permit is to speak with the relevant code official. The code official will make some general inquiries, and may make recommendations regarding restrictions in the planned building area. After this interview, the code official will provide the application for a building permit. This application will require the location, planned structure, schedule, payment protocol, and construction plan for the project. Any sketches or architectural plans that have been created must be included with the application. The code official then reviews the application and either grants or denies the permit. If the permit is denied, the code official may offer suggestions. There is a fee, which varies depending on the project scale, for the review of the application.

Job-site visits

After a building permit has been issued, the state of California will still send an inspector to the job site to ensure that work is being performed according to the permit plans. Also, the inspector acts as a resource for the builder, who may not be familiar with the minutiae of the California Building Code. The presence of the inspector can prevent expensive mistakes. The inspector usually gives the builder an estimate of how many inspections will be required. In some cases, the builder will ask for an inspection to settle a particular question. It is typical for the inspector to require a day's notice before such a visit.

Plan review and permit expiration

If an application is submitted and no permit is issued for 180 days, the application expires. The applicant must then resubmit the plans and pay a small fee for an extension. This extension will have the same duration as the original application. If an application has been expired for six months, it cannot be resubmitted. Once a permit has been issued, there are still two scenarios under which it can expire. If the work outlined in the permit is not begun within 180 days of the permit's issuance, the permit expires. A renewed permit then must be obtained before work can begin. Also, a permit can be revoked if a building official determines that it has been issued wrongly.

Appeals procedure

Sometimes, a would-be builder will want to appeal the decision of a building official. To do this, a written appeal must be filed within ten days of the decision. This appeal must lay out in great detail the reasons for the appeal. The secretary of the board of appeals will then call a board meeting for some time within the next thirty days,

Copyright © Mometrix Media. You have been licensed one copy of this document for personal use only. Any other reproduction or redistribution is strictly prohibited. All rights reserved.

though the appellant will have at least ten days' warning of the upcoming meeting. At the meeting, the board of appeals will render judgment and mail a copy of the decision to the appellant within the next thirty days.

Uniform codes

Uniform codes have been developed to align the statutes of different states, with the aim of facilitating interstate commerce. The most important uniform code is the Uniform Commercial Code, which directly centers on commercial transactions between the states. The Uniform Commercial Code is not itself law, but is issued as recommendations to the state legislatures. This and other uniform codes must be approved by the California state legislature. The state of California has made only miniscule changes to the Uniform Commercial Code, though the state has implemented some changes with regard to the manner in which the Code is organized. In California, the major subdivisions of the Uniform Commercial Code are called divisions rather than articles. Furthermore, California does not use hyphens in section numbers, because the state uses hyphens to indicate a range of divisions.

Field changes

Sometimes, a builder discovers only after receiving a permit that some of the proposed materials and methods are unsuitable. It is possible to have alternate materials and methods approved without entirely scrapping the original permit. However, it is necessary for the builder to submit a request for field changes. This request will be reviewed in a timely fashion by a building official. So long as the proposed changes do not diminish the strength, effectiveness, durability, safety, sanitation, and fire resistance of the structure, they are likely to be approved. The builder should not begin work related to these changes until the alternate materials and methods request has been approved.

Essential services buildings

In the state of California, an essential services building is defined as any structure used for public agencies, as for instance emergency communications dispatch centers, police stations, and fire houses. Such buildings have special design requirements so that they will be more likely to withstand natural disasters, in particular earthquakes, mudslides, and high winds. It is very important that these building remain standing and operational during emergencies. The design requirements for essential services buildings are essentially the highest outlined in the California Building Code.

Building code

The set of provisions that govern the construction and design of structures in the state of California is known as the California Building Code, Title 24, Parts 2, Volume 1 and 2. An interior designer will need to reference this work often during his or her

Copyright © Mometrix Media. You have been licensed one copy of this document for personal use only. Any other reproduction or redistribution is strictly prohibited. All rights reserved.

professional practice, so it is important to understand its organizational structure. To begin with, the Code is divided into two volumes because of its size. These volumes are divided into chapters. Chapter 2 of the Code is devoted to general definitions of the terms that will appear frequently in the rest of the Code. Terms that do not appear in this chapter may be defined in a special definitions section within a particular chapter. Each chapter is divided into sections. The sections appear in numerical order, with the first number being the chapter number. So, for instance, the first section in Chapter 4 is Section 401. Within these titled sections, the regulations are laid out in full. Often, the regulations in one section will refer to another section of the Code.

Finding building code definitions

The state of California has established specific definitions for key terms within the Building Code. In order to understand the provisions of the Code, an interior designer needs to be able to find definitions quickly. Luckily, this process has been made easy by the organization of the Code. For starters, Chapter 2 in Volume 1 of the Code is entirely devoted to general definitions. Also, many of the subsequent chapters in the Code have sections listing the definitions of the key terms for that section. For instance, Chapter 8 is devoted to interior finishes, and Section 802 defines all of the key terms related to that subject.

Copyright © Mometrix Media. You have been licensed one copy of this document for personal use only. Any other reproduction or redistribution is strictly prohibited. All rights reserved.

Occupancy

Occupancy Group A

In the California Building Code, all of the A groups are for assembly buildings--buildings in which large numbers of people gather together. There are five different groups within this occupancy class.

- A-1: Fixed-seating structures used for the viewing of performance arts or motion pictures. Examples include movie theatres, sound stages, theatres, symphony halls, and concert halls.
- A-2: Buildings in which large numbers of people gather to consumer food or drinks. Examples include bars, restaurants, night clubs, and banquet halls.
- A-3: Places for religious worship, recreation or amusement. Examples include art galleries, dance halls, community halls, churches, mosques, synagogues, courtrooms, funeral parlors, libraries, museums, and pool halls.
- A-4: Buildings used for indoor sporting events, with seating for spectators. Examples include arenas, skating rinks, and indoor tennis courts.
- A-5: Buildings used for participation in outdoor activities. Examples include bleachers, stadiums, and amusement park seating structures.

Occupancy Groups B and E

In the California Building Code, occupancy group B is for business structures. In other words, these are buildings in which professional services are performed. Some examples of group B structures are offices, motor vehicle showrooms, dry cleaners, car washes, beauty shops, banks, and radio stations. Occupancy group E is for educational structures. If any part of a building is used for the education of more than six people at or below the twelfth grade at any given time, it is considered to be part of occupancy group E. Buildings used for religious education are typically included in A-3. Day cares, however, are classified in group E so long as there are more than six children older than 2.5 years old.

Occupancy Groups F-1 and F-2

In the California Building Code, occupancy group F is for factories. Group F facilities are any in which assembling, disassembling, fabricating, finishing, manufacturing, packaging, repair, or processing takes place. The buildings in this category are subdivided into F-1 and F-2, depending on whether they are low or moderate hazard. F-1 buildings are moderate hazard occupancies. They include operations related to aircraft, appliances, bicycles, carpets, clothing, electronics, furniture, food processing, soaps, printing, or woodworking. F-2 buildings are low-hazard occupancies. They perform operations on things like ceramics, metal, ice, glass, and brick.

Copyright © Mometrix Media. You have been licensed one copy of this document for personal use only. Any other reproduction or redistribution is strictly prohibited. All rights reserved.

Occupancy Groups H and I

In the California Building Code, occupancy group H is for buildings in which high-hazard operations are performed. In other words, these are buildings where hazardous materials are manufactured, stored, processed, or generated. There are five subcategories, H-1 through H-5, distinguished by the type of hazard they present to the general public. Occupancy group I is for institutional buildings, or buildings in which people are supervised or treated. There are four subcategories. In I-1 buildings people are housed all day and night. In I-2 buildings people stay all day and night so that medical, nursing, or psychiatric services can be performed for them. In I-3 buildings, people are held under restraint. I-4 buildings are daycare facilities.

Occupancy Groups M and U

In the California Building Code, occupancy group M is for mercantile buildings. These are structures accessible to the public, in which goods are displayed and sold. Some examples of group M buildings include drug stores, department stores, retail stores, wholesale stores, markets, and gas stations. There are restrictions on the amount of hazardous material that can be stored in a group M building. Occupancy group U is for utility and miscellaneous structures. This is basically a catch-all category for the structures that do not fit into one of the other occupancy groups. These include sheds, greenhouses, aircraft hangars, grain silos, towers, barns, carports, and private garages.

Occupancy Group R

In the California Building Code, occupancy group R is for residential structures. This basically encompasses all of the buildings that people sleep in that are not in group I. There are four subcategories of occupancy group R. Group R-1 buildings contain sleeping spots for transient people. Examples of R-1 buildings include boarding houses and hotels. R-2 buildings contain multiple sleeping and dwelling units for primarily permanent occupants. Some examples of R-2 structures are apartment buildings, convents, dormitories, fraternity houses, and timeshares. R-3 structures are residential occupancies for primarily permanent residents, including non-townhouses that contain less than three dwelling units, townhouses with a separate means of egress that are less than three stories, and care facilities. R-4 occupancies are residential care/assisted living buildings, so long as they house more than six ambulatory clients.

Occupancy Group S

In the state of California Building Code, the structures in occupancy group S are used for storage, so long as what is being stored is not a hazardous material. Occupancy group S is divided into two subcategories. S-1 occupancies are used to store the

Copyright © Mometrix Media. You have been licensed one copy of this document for personal use only. Any other reproduction or redistribution is strictly prohibited. All rights reserved.

following sorts of materials: aerosols, bags, baskets, books, boots, shoes, clothing, furniture, grain, lumber, silk, soap, sugar, tobacco, and upholstery. S-2 buildings are used to store noncombustible materials, particularly those that are placed on wooden pallets or packaged in paper. Some of the products commonly housed in S-2 buildings are beverages, cement, food, electrical supplies, glass, mirrors, pottery, stoves, and metal.

Zoning restrictions

Interior designers need to be familiar with the zoning conditions and covenants that apply in their jurisdiction, in particular when they are deciding whether to operate out of a home office. For one thing, there may be zoning restrictions in place which will forbid home offices. However, it is possible on occasion to obtain a zoning variance which allows the operation of a business in a residential area. This is usually possible if the designer can demonstrate that his or her business will not disrupt the tranquility of the neighborhood. Finally, in some cases the conditions, covenants and restrictions of a neighborhood will forbid a home-based business. An interior designer should investigate these issues in his or her own neighborhood before considering a home-based business.

Copyright © Mometrix Media. You have been licensed one copy of this document for personal use only. Any other reproduction or redistribution is strictly prohibited. All rights reserved.

Construction Types

Allowable heights and usable areas for Groups: A-1, A-2, and A-3

The state of California has produced a comprehensive table outlining the allowable heights and usable areas for all occupancy groups and construction types. The following table covers groups A-1, A-2, and A-3. Height in stories is first, followed by area in square feet. Construction type is listed along the top, and occupancy group along the left side. UL stands for unlimited.

	I-A	I-B	II-A	II-B	III-A
A-1	UL; UL	5; UL	3; 15,500	2; 8500	3; 14,000
A-2	UL; UL	11; UL	3; 15,500	2; 8500	3; 14,000
A-3	UL; UL	11; UL	3; 15,500	2; 9500	3; 14,000

	III-B	IV	V-A	V-B
A-1	2; 8500	3; 15,000	2; 11,500	1; 5500
A-2	2; 9500	3; 15,000	2; 11,500	1; 6000
A-3	2; 9500	3; 15,000	2; 11,500	1; 6000

Allowable heights and usable areas for Groups: A-4, A-5, and B

The state of California has produced a comprehensive table outlining the allowable heights and usable areas for all occupancy groups and construction types. The following table covers groups A-4, A-5, and B. Height in stories is first, followed by area in square feet. Construction type is listed along the top, and occupancy group along the left side. UL stands for unlimited.

	I-A	I-B	II-A	II-B	III-A
A-4	UL; UL	11; UL	315,500	29,500	314,000
A-5	UL; UL	UL;UL	UL; UL	UL; UL	UL; UL
B	UL; UL	11; UL	5; 37,500	4; 23,000	5; 28,500

	III-B	IV	V-A	V-B
A-4	29,500	315,000	2; 11,500	1; 6000
A-5	UL; UL	UL; UL	UL; UL	UL; UL
B	4; 19,000	5; 36,000	3; 18,000	29,000

Copyright © Mometrix Media. You have been licensed one copy of this document for personal use only. Any other reproduction or redistribution is strictly prohibited. All rights reserved.

Allowable heights and usable areas for Groups: E, F-1, and F-2

The state of California has produced a comprehensive table outlining the allowable heights and usable areas for all occupancy groups and construction types. The following table covers groups E, F-1, and F-2. Height in stories is first, followed by area in square feet. Construction type is listed along the top, and occupancy group along the left side. UL stands for unlimited.

	I-A	I-B	II-A	II-B	III-A
E	UL; UL	5; UL	3; 26,500	2; 14,500	3; 23,500
F-1	UL; UL	11; UL	4; 25,000	2; 15,500	3; 19,000
F-2	UL; UL	11; UL	5; 37,500	3; 23,000	4; 28,500

	III-B	IV	V-A	V-B
E	2; 14,500	3; 25,500	1; 18,500	1; 9500
F-1	2; 12,000	4; 33,500	2; 14,000	1; 8500
F-2	3; 18,000	5; 50,500	3; 21,000	2; 13,000

Allowable heights and usable areas for Groups: H-1, H-2, and H-3

The state of California has produced a comprehensive table outlining the allowable heights and usable areas for all occupancy groups and construction types. The following table covers groups H-1, H-2, and H-3. Height in stories is first, followed by area in square feet. Construction type is listed along the top, and occupancy group along the left side. UL stands for unlimited. NA stands for not allowed.

	I-A	I-B	II-A	II-B
H-1	1; 21,000	1; 16,500	1; 11,000	1; 7000
H-2	UL; 21,000	3; 16,500	2; 11,000	1; 7000
H-3	UL; UL	6; 60,000	426,500	214,000

	III-A	III-B	IV	V-A	V-B
H-1	1; 9500	1; 7000	1; 10,500	1; 7500	NA
H-2	2; 9500	1; 7000	2; 10,500	1; 7500	1; 3000
H-3	417,500	213,000	425,500	2; 10,000	1; 5000

Copyright © Mometrix Media. You have been licensed one copy of this document for personal use only. Any other reproduction or redistribution is strictly prohibited. All rights reserved.

Allowable heights and usable areas for Groups: H-4, H-5, and I-1

The state of California has produced a comprehensive table outlining the allowable heights and usable areas for all occupancy groups and construction types. The following table covers groups H-4, H-5, and I-1. Height in stories is first, followed by area in square feet. Construction type is listed along the top, and occupancy group along the left side. UL stands for unlimited.

	I-A	I-B	II-A	II-B	III-A
H-4	UL; UL	7; UL	5; 37,500	3; 17,500	5; 28,500
H-5	4; UL	4; UL	3; 37,500	3; 23,000	3; 28,500
I-1	UL; UL	9; 55,000	4; 19,000	3; 10,000	4; 16,500

	III-B	IV	V-A	V-B
H-4	3; 17,500	5; 36,000	3; 18,000	2; 6500
H-5	3; 19,000	3; 36,000	3; 18,000	2; 9000
I-1	3; 10,000	4; 18,000	3; 10,500	2; 4500

Allowable heights and usable areas for Groups: I-2, I-3, and I-4

The state of California has produced a comprehensive table outlining the allowable heights and usable areas for all occupancy groups and construction types. The following table covers groups I-2, I-3, and I-4. Height in stories is first, followed by area in square feet. Construction type is listed along the top, and occupancy group along the left side. UL stands for unlimited. NA stands for not allowed.

	I-A	I-B	II-A	II-B	III-A
I-2	UL; UL	4; UL	2; 15,000	1; 11,000	1; 12,000
I-3	UL; UL	2; 15,100	NA	NA	NA
I-4	UL; UL	5; 60,500	3; 26,500	2; 13,000	3; 23,500

	III-B	IV	V-A	V-B
I-2	NA	1; 12,000	1; 9500	NA
I-3	NA	NA	NA	NA
I-4	2; 13,000	3; 23,500	1; 18,500	1; 9000

Copyright © Mometrix Media. You have been licensed one copy of this document for personal use only. Any other reproduction or redistribution is strictly prohibited. All rights reserved.

Allowable heights and usable areas for Groups: L, M, and R-1

The state of California has produced a comprehensive table outlining the allowable heights and usable areas for all occupancy groups and construction types. The following table covers groups L, M, and R-1. Height in stories is first, followed by area in square feet. Construction type is listed along the top, and occupancy group along the left side. UL stands for unlimited.

	I-A	I-B	II-A	II-B
L	10; UL	3; 39,900	3; 18,000	2; 12,000
M	UL; UL	11; UL	4; 21,500	4; 12,500
R-1	UL; UL	11; UL	4; 24,000	4; 16,000

	III-A	III-B	IV	V-A	V-B
L	3; 18,000	2; 12,000	3; 18,000	3; 14,000	1; 8000
M	4; 18,500	4; 12,500	4; 20,500	3; 14,000	1; 9000
R-1	4; 24,000	4; 16,000	4; 20,500	3; 12,000	2; 7000

Allowable heights and usable areas for Groups: R-2, R-3, and R-4

The state of California has produced a comprehensive table outlining the allowable heights and usable areas for all occupancy groups and construction types. The following table covers groups R-2, R-3, and R-4. Height in stories is first, followed by area in square feet. Construction type is listed along the top, and occupancy group along the left side. UL stands for unlimited.

	I-A	I-B	II-A	II-B
R-2	UL; UL	11; UL	4; 24,000	4; 16,000
R-3	UL; UL	11; UL	4; UL	4; UL
R-4	UL; UL	11; UL	4; 24,000	4; 16,000

	III-A	III-B	IV	V-A	V-B
R-2	4; 24,000	4; 16,000	4; 20,500	3; 12,000	2; 7000
R-3	4; UL	4; UL	4; UL	3; UL	3; UL
R-4	4; 24,000	4; 16,000	4; 20,500	3; 12,000	2; 7000

Copyright © Mometrix Media. You have been licensed one copy of this document for personal use only. Any other reproduction or redistribution is strictly prohibited. All rights reserved.

, and usable areas for Groups: S-1, S-2, and U

_ornia has produced a comprehensive table outlining the allowable _ble areas for all occupancy groups and construction types. The _e covers groups S-1, S-2, and U. Height in stories is first, followed by _e feet. Construction type is listed along the top, and occupancy group _t side. UL stands for unlimited.

	I-A	I-B	II-A	II-B
S-1	UL; UL	11; 48,000	4; 26,000	3; 17,500
S-2	UL; UL	11; 79,000	5; 39,000	4; 26,000
U	UL; UL	5; 35,500	4; 19,000	2; 8500

	III-A	III-B	IV	V-A	V-B
S-1	3; 26,000	3; 17,500	4; 25,500	3; 14,000	1; 9000
S-2	4; 39,000	4; 26,000	5; 38,500	4; 21,000	2; 13,500
U	3; 14,000	2; 8500	4; 18,000	2; 9000	1; 5500

Construction type classifications

In order to simplify the fire-resistance classification of buildings according to construction type, the IBC has established five classes. They are labeled I through V, with Type I having the highest fire resistance. Some of these classes are further divided into A and B subgroups, which indicate whether the building is fire-protected. This classification system makes it easy for interior designers to determine what sort of changes will need to be made in order to accommodate a given design scheme. For instance, a designer will know whether or not a comprehensive sprinkler system is mandated, which will help in designing an appropriate ceiling

Construction Types I, II, and III

In the state of California, building construction is divided into five types. Types I and II construction are very similar. Most of the building elements in these structures must be noncombustible, though there are some exceptions. For instance, Type I construction must have a structural frame and bearing walls with a fire-resistance rating of at least 2. Type II construction, on the other hand, need not have fire-resistance rating higher than 0 for these elements. In Type III construction, the outside walls are made of noncombustible materials, though the interior walls need not be. If an exterior wall assembly has a two-hour rating or less, some fire-retardant-treated wood frames can be used in Type III construction.

Copyright © Mometrix Media. You have been licensed one copy of this document for personal use only. Any other reproduction or redistribution is strictly prohibited. All rights reserved.

Construction Type IV

Type IV construction, also known as Heavy Timber (or HT) construction, has noncombustible exterior walls and interior elements composed of solid or laminated wood without hidden spaces. The wood columns used in Type IV construction must be glued laminated or sawn, and they cannot be less than six inches in any direction when supporting a floor load, and not less than eight by six inches when only supporting a roof and ceiling. As for floor framing, wood beams and girders have to be made of sawn or glue-laminated timber. These elements must be at least six inches wide and ten inches deep. A framed timber truss supporting a floor load must be at least eight inches in every dimension.

In Type IV construction, if the roof is made out of wood-frame or glued-laminated arches that originate at the floor load, the members should be at least 6 inches wide and 8 inches deep on the bottom, and at least 6 inches deep on the top. If the roof is made of framed or glued-laminated arches that originate in the top of the wall or the wall abutment, the members must be at least 4 inches side and 6 inches deep. If the members are spaced, they can be made up of two or more pieces at least three inches thick. Splice plates have to be at least three inches thick. When framing timbers are protected by automatic sprinklers underneath a roof deck, the members have to be at least 3 inches wide.

In Type IV construction, there cannot be any concealed space in the floor. There are special requirements for wooden floors. They must be composed of sawn or glued-laminated planks, either splinted or tongue-and-groove, at least three inches thick. There should not be any continuous joint lines except at support points. The floor should not come within half an inch of the wall, with this gap being covered by a molding. Wooden floors are apt to swell or shrink, and it is important that the molding not block this movement. Instead of molding, a designer can opt for corbelling of the masonry walls underneath the floor.

In Type IV construction, there are three possible ways for partitions to be constructed. They may be composed of one-hour fire-resistance-rated construction, four-inch-thick laminated construction, or solid wood construction composed of at least two layers of one-inch-thick matched boards. The exterior structural members of Type IV construction must conform to the heavy timber sizes if there is a horizontal separation of at least twenty feet.

Construction Type V

The standards for Type V construction are very loose; the structural elements, exterior walls, and interior walls of Type V construction may be composed of any materials permitted by the California Building ode.

Copyright © Mometrix Media. You have been licensed one copy of this document for personal use only. Any other reproduction or redistribution is strictly prohibited. All rights reserved.

Wall and fire wall requirements

The fire resistance rating of exterior walls is specified in Tables 601 and 602 of the California Building Code. If the fire separation distance of the exterior walls is more than five feet, the walls must be rated for exposure to internal fire. If the fire separation distance is less than five feet, the walls are rated for exposure to internal and external fire. The California Building Code lays out specific requirements for the area of exterior wall openings. In some cases, such openings are not permitted. Fire walls, meanwhile, must be stable enough to stay upright even when construction on either side has collapsed. Fire walls in occupancy groups A, B, E, H-4, I, R-1, R-2, U, F-1, H-3, H-5, M, S-1, and L must have a fire-resistance rating of 3 hours. Fire walls in occupancy groups H-1 and H-2 must have a fire-resistance rating of 4 hours. Fire walls in occupancy groups F-2, S-2, R-3, and R-4 must have a fire-resistance rating of 2 hours.

Upholstered furniture flammability requirements and testing procedures

California Technical Bulletin 116 outlines the requirements and the testing procedures for the flammability of upholstered furniture. Flammability is tested by applying a lit cigarette to a piece of standard upholstered furniture. The furniture is considered to fail the test if it combusts or if char develops any more than two inches from the lit end of the cigarette. Also, upholstered furniture needs to maintain its flame retardant capabilities despite changes in temperature, humidity, and use. The tests performed by the state of California are sure to use normal pieces of furniture in normal conditions. Each different part of the furniture must be tested separately. The general intention is to test furniture as it is sold and as it will be used.

The tests performed to measure the flammability of upholstered furniture are detailed in California Technical Bulletin 116. In the smooth surface and decking tests, three lit cigarettes are placed on a smooth part of the furniture. The cigarettes are allowed to burn their full length, and should not lie across a tuft or stitching. In a welt test, three lit cigarettes are placed in the depression created by a welt. The cigarettes should be placed parallel to the welt. In some cases, it may be necessary to hold the cigarettes in place with a straight pin. In a quilted location test, three cigarettes are placed on quilted parts of the furniture. They should be arranged such that they will burn down into the quilted depression.

The tests performed to measure the flammability of upholstered furniture are detailed in California Technical Bulletin 116. In the tufted location test, three lit cigarettes are placed on tufted parts of the furniture. The cigarettes should be arranged such that they will burn down into the tuft depression. Also, the butt ends

Copyright © Mometrix Media. You have been licensed one copy of this document for personal use only. Any other reproduction or redistribution is strictly prohibited. All rights reserved.

of the cigarettes should be arranged such that they burn out over the buttons or laces of the tufts. When a piece of upholstered furniture has crevices, such as those related to panels or cushions, three lit cigarettes should be placed in the crevice between the cushion/panel and upholstery. Also, when a piece of furniture has arms or backs (a chair, for instance), three burning cigarettes should be placed atop these locations.

Flammability requirements for mattresses used in high risk occupancies

The flammability requirements for mattresses used in high-risk occupancies are outlined in California Technical Bulletin 121. High-risk occupancies include jails, prisons, nursing homes, and health care facilities. The test described in Technical Bulletin 121 is different than the one used for residential mattresses. A full-size mattress is used in the test. In the test, ten sheets of newspaper are wadded up and placed in a galvanized metal container, such that the newspaper is even with the top of the container. The mattress is placed in a horizontal position on top of some device capable of measuring its weight. A thermocouple is placed one inch below the ceiling and directly above the center of the mattress.

Once the mattress has been arranged properly, the container filled with newspaper should be placed underneath its center. The bottom of the mattress should be about three inches above the top of the container. The newspaper is then ignited with a match, and the whole system is allowed to burn until it goes out or at least ten percent of the mattress' weight has been consumed. A mattress fails the test if it loses more than ten percent of its weight in the first ten minutes, if the combustion reaches a temperature of 500 degrees Fahrenheit or greater, or if the concentration of carbon monoxide exceeds 1000 parts per million at any time.

Flammability test procedures for seating furniture used in public occupancies

The procedures for testing the flammability of seating furniture used in public occupancies are outlined in California Technical Bulletin 133. Public occupancies are exemplified by prisons, nursing homes, auditoriums, and hotels, though other buildings may qualify as public occupancies as well. The test outlined in Bulletin 133 is not the one used on residential furniture. The furniture sample used in the test should be conditioned and prepared just as it would be for normal use. It should include all of the parts that such a piece of furniture would require. During the test, thermocouples should be placed in two different locations. One should be placed over the geometric center of the ignition source, one inch underneath the ceiling. Another should be placed three feet in front of the ignition source and four feet underneath the ceiling.

Before beginning the flammability test for seating furniture to be used in public occupancies, a smoke opacity monitor should be placed four feet above the floor. A gas sampling line should be placed 6.5 inches from the intersection of two walls and 6.5 inches below the ceiling. The furniture should be placed on a platform capable of

Copyright © Mometrix Media. You have been licensed one copy of this document for personal use only. Any other reproduction or redistribution is strictly prohibited. All rights reserved.

weight. This platform should be about 5.2 inches above the floor. The ~~)uld~~ be within ten inches of two of the walls. The placement of the ~~ice~~, a square gas burner, depends on the width of the furniture. If the ~~; more~~ than 40 inches wide, the burner should be placed five inches from ~~m crevice~~ or edge of the seat. If the furniture is less than 40 inches wide, ~~the~~ ~~er~~ should be placed in the middle of the crevice area, one inch above the seat surface, and two inches from the back of the piece of furniture.

The procedures for testing the flammability of seating furniture to be used in public occupancies are outlined in Technical Bulletin 133. Once the test begins, the square gas burner should be ignited for about eighty seconds. The test should continue uninterrupted until one of the following three conditions is met: combustion has ceased, one hour has elapsed, or flameover/flashover seemingly cannot be avoided. There are a number of ways that a piece of furniture can fail the test. If the ceiling thermocouple ever registers a temperature of 200 degrees Fahrenheit or more, the furniture fails the test. If the four-foot thermocouple ever registers a temperature increase of more than 50 degrees Fahrenheit, the furniture fails the test.

If during the test the four-foot-high smoke opacity monitor registers greater than 75% opacity, the piece of furniture has failed the test. If the carbon monoxide concentration in the room ever exceeds 1000 parts per million for longer than five minutes, the furniture fails the test. The furniture also fails the test if it loses more than three pounds during the first ten minutes of the test. Sometimes, the test is performed with oxygen consumption calorimetry equipment instead of the above-mentioned gear. If oxygen consumption calorimetry equipment is used, the furniture fails when any of the following four conditions are met: total heat release of more than 24 MJ during the first ten minutes of the test, greater than 75% opacity recorded by the four-foot-high smoke opacity monitor, maximum rate of heat release more than 79kW, or carbon monoxide concentration of 1000 parts per million or more for at least five minutes.

Flammability test procedures for mattresses used in public buildings

The procedures for testing the flammability of mattresses used in public buildings are outlined in California Technical Bulletin 129. In California, public buildings include nursing homes, college dormitories, and prisons. The test measures the combustion and heat release when the mattress is subjected to flame. The mattress is ignited with a propane gas burner. There is a weighing platform under the mattress, so that the weight loss due to combustion can be measured. There is also equipment for measuring the rate of heat and smoke release and the rate and concentration of carbon oxides release. A mattress is considered to have failed the test if any of the following three conditions are met: the mattress loses three pounds in the first ten minutes of the test, the heat release meets or exceeds 100 kW, or there is a total heat release of 25 MJ or more in the first ten minutes of the test.

Copyright © Mometrix Media. You have been licensed one copy of this document for personal use only. Any other reproduction or redistribution is strictly prohibited. All rights reserved.

Flammability standards tests

The following tests are routinely applied to interior design components to determine degree of flammability:

- Vertical ignition test: A pass/fail test that is applied to draperies, curtains, and window dressings. This test measures the degree to which a flame will spread when the surface of the fabric is ignited.
- Cigarette ignition resistance test of furniture components: Tests the flammability of various cushions and furniture parts in response to cigarettes and open flames.
- Cigarette ignition resistance test of furniture composites: Tests the flammability of a seat cushion, liner, and fabric to a lit cigarette.
- Full seating test: Tests the flammability of a fully assembled and upholstered chair in contact with an open flame.

Furniture fabric flammability testing

The makers of furniture fabric are required to subject their products to a great deal of flammability testing before it can be sold to interior designers and their clients. In order to purchase safe fabrics, interior designers need to be familiar with some of the terminology around this subject. For instance, char is any material that is left over after an incomplete combustion. Some fabrics will burn up completely, while others will leave behind char. A flame-retardant is any substance which is capable of impeding the growth and expansion of a fire. Some fabrics are flame-retardant. Finally, smoldering is the ignition of a substance in which there is no open flame, but rather smoke, toxic gas and heat. Smoldering materials pose a significant threat to the user, despite the absence of fire.

Copyright © Mometrix Media. You have been licensed one copy of this document for personal use only. Any other reproduction or redistribution is strictly prohibited. All rights reserved.

Interior Finish

Interior finish materials

The California Building Code outlines specific provisions related to interior finish materials, trim, and decorative materials. The allowable flame spread and smoke-developed indices depend on the location and the occupancy classification. The flame spread index is a measure of the distance a flame will travel from its source in a given amount of time. The smoke-developed index is a measure of how much smoke will obscure the air over a given amount of time. In general, it is alright to use combustible materials as finish for walls, ceilings, and floors, but these materials must be within the allowed limits for flame spread and the development of smoke.

Classification of wall and ceiling finishes

In the California Building Code, wall and ceiling finishes are divided into three classes, according to their flame-spread index. Class A materials have a flame spread index between 0 and 25 (there are no units for this measure). Class B materials have a flame spread index between 26 and 75. Class C materials have a flame spread index between 76 and 200. All of these materials must have a smoke-developed index of less than 451. Wall and ceiling finishes that are not made of textiles must be subjected to a 40 kW and 160 kW exposures, during which flame spread must be minimal. All wall and ceiling finishes must stay attached even when room temperatures are 200 degrees Fahrenheit or greater for thirty minutes or more.

Requirements for the application of wall and ceiling finish

The California Building Code outlines specific provisions for the application of wall and ceiling finish. In some cases, a wall or ceiling is required to meet noncombustible or fire-resistant standards. When this is true, the interior finish should either be directly applied or attached to furring strips no more than 1 ¾ inches thick. If, moreover, the interior finish materials are being used in set-out constriction, Class A finish materials are required. In heavy timber construction, all classes of wall and ceiling finish are acceptable. In general, interior finish materials less than a quarter-inch thick should be applied directly to a noncombustible backing. The only exceptions to this general proviso are Class A materials and materials that were not tested directly against the backing.

Classification and requirements for interior floor finish

In California, interior floor finishes are separated into two classes, depending on their critical radiant flux (the distance the floor will burn before it extinguishes itself): Class I (0.45 watts/cm2 or more) and Class II (0.22 watts/cm2 or more). The interior finish must be at least Class I in occupancy groups I-2, and at least Class II in

- 18 -

Copyright © Mometrix Media. You have been licensed one copy of this document for personal use only. Any other reproduction or redistribution is strictly prohibited. All rights reserved.

groups A, B, E, H, I-4, M, R-1, R-2, and S. If a building other than I-3 has a sprinkler system, than Class II materials are allowed. In an I-3 where the occupants are being restrained (i.e., a mental institution or prison), interior floor finish must be noncombustible.

Application of combustible floor finish in Type I or II construction

The rules for the application of combustible floor finish in Type I or II construction vary depending on the type of flooring. For instance, in subfloor construction, bucks, nailing blocks, and floor sleepers should not be made of combustible materials. Wood finish flooring, on the other hand, can be attached directly to fire-blocked or embedded wooden sleepers. Also, wooden finish flooring can be attached directly to the top of fire-resistance-rated floor construction or a wood subfloor connected to sleepers. Designers are allowed to use combustible insulating boards no more than a half-inch thick, so long as they are covered with an approved floor finish and connected directly a noncombustible floor assembly or wood subflooring with attached sleepers.

Copyright © Mometrix Media. You have been licensed one copy of this document for personal use only. Any other reproduction or redistribution is strictly prohibited. All rights reserved.

Means of Egress

Egress system

A means of egress is simply a clear, unblocked path from any point in a building to a public way. A public way is any street or other piece of land that is clear from ground to sky, is a minimum of **10 feet wide**, and is permanently allotted for public use. In order to be complete, a means of egress must contain exit access, an exit, and an exit discharge. The exit access is the part of the building that leads to the exit. The exit is the path that leads from the exit access to the exit discharge. It can be a door, stairway, or corridor. The exit discharge is the path from the exit to the public way. It might be a balcony or a courtyard.

Occupant load requirements

In order for a building to remain safe, a designer needs to know the occupant load of the space. Occupant load is the number of people who will be staying in or moving through a given space. The occupant load of a space is calculated by dividing the total area in square feet by the occupant load factor. The occupant load factor is the amount of floor space that a building code assumes to be occupied by a single person in a given occupancy. The occupant load factor will change depending on who is to occupy the space, as well as what the occupants will be doing there.

Ceiling height and headroom requirements

The state of California has established specific provisions for means of egress. The ceiling of a means of egress must be at least 7 foot 6 inches tall. There must be at least 80 inches of headroom above any walking surface. Walking surfaces include sidewalks, hallways, aisles, and passageways. Also, no more than half of the ceiling area in a means of egress can feature protruding objects. If the vertical clearance in a means of egress is any less than 80 inches, there must be a barrier, with the leading edge of the barrier at most 27 inches above the floor.

Freestanding object and horizontal projection requirements

If there is a freestanding object mounted on a post, it may not hang over the post any more than 4 inches, so long as the leading edge of the post is between 27 and 80 inches above the floor. On the other hand, if the object is mounted between posts that are farther apart, the lowest edge of the object must be between 27 and 80 inches above the floor. The state of California declares that structural elements and fixtures may not jut out over a floor more than 4 inches between the heights of 27 and 80 inches above the floor.

Copyright © Mometrix Media. You have been licensed one copy of this document for personal use only. Any other reproduction or redistribution is strictly prohibited. All rights reserved.

Floor surface and elevation change requirements

In the state of California, the floor or walking surface in a means of egress has to be firmly attached and has to have some sort of slip-resistant surface. If the floor of the means of egress changes less than one foot, a sloped surface is required. If the difference in elevation is no more than 6 inches, the sloped surface needs to have handrails or a contrasting floor finish. Moreover, any elevation change that is designed for non-ambulatory persons needs to be sloped.

Continuity, elevator, escalator, and moving walk requirements

In the state of California, the Building Code asserts that nothing other than an authorized means of egress component is allowed to interrupt the path of egress travel. When there are obstructions in the path, they must not violate capacity requirements. In general, the carrying capacity of a means of egress may not be diminished by obstruction. The required means of egress from any part of a building may not feature elevators, escalators, and moving walks. These structural elements are considered too risky for a means of egress.

Maximum floor area allowances

The state of California establishes a maximum floor area allowance per occupant in common occupancy areas. For an interior designer, the most important are the following: assembly without fixed seats, concentrated (7 net); assembly without fixed seats, standing space (5 net); assembly without fixed seats, unconcentrated (15 net); business area (100 gross); daycare (35 net); classroom (20 net); vocational classroom (50 net); inpatient treatment areas (240 gross); outpatient area (100 gross); sleeping areas, institutional (120 gross); commercial kitchens (200 gross); library reading room (15 net); library stack area (100 gross); residential (200 gross); mercantile, areas on other floors (60 gross); mercantile, basement and grade floor areas (30 gross); mercantile, storage, stock, shipping areas (300 gross); and warehouse (500 gross).

Occupant load

The state of California has outlined strict standards for occupant load in a means of egress. In situations where people are entering an egress area from an accessory area by means of a primary space, the calculator of occupant load in the primary space combines the total occupant load and the occupant load of the accessory area. In an area without fixed seating, there can only be one occupant per prescribed unit of area. Moreover, the occupant load cannot be any less than the quotient of the floor area and the maximum occupancy allowance.

If the occupant load is no greater than one occupant per 7 square feet of floor space, and all the other requirements of the Building Code related to occupant load are met, the occupant load may be allowed to increase. The designer must submit for a

Copyright © Mometrix Media. You have been licensed one copy of this document for personal use only. Any other reproduction or redistribution is strictly prohibited. All rights reserved.

permit to the building official. The occupant load of any assembly space must be posted in plain sight; close to the main exit or to the exit access doorway. Such a sign must be legible, and must be maintained by the owner of the building. In some cases, an exit serves more than one floor. As long as the exit capacity is not diminished in the direction of the egress travel, the occupant load of each floor is considered individually.

In areas with fixed seating, the occupant load depends on the number of fixed seats. If the seats do not have dividing arms, the occupant load has to be more than the number of seats, given 18 inches of seating length per person. In a restaurant or other area with booths, each person must be allotted 2 feet of seat length. In outdoor areas, for instance patios and courts, the occupant load is typically added on to the occupant load of the adjoining building. If the outdoor area is only used for servicing the building, it only needs to have one means of egress.

Egress width requirements

There are specific provisions for the width of an egress system both with and without sprinklers. In almost all occupancies, there must be 0.3 inches of stairway width per person and 0.2 inches of width for other egress components per person if there is no sprinkler system. If there is a sprinkler system, there must be 0.2 inches of stairway width per occupant, and 0.15 inches of width for other egress components per person. The only exception to these requirements that is important for interior designers is in I-2 institutional spaces, which, when serviced by a sprinkler, must have 0.3 inches per occupant in the stairways and 0.2 inches per occupant for other egress components.

Illumination requirements

In the state of California, all parts of the means of egress, including the exit discharge, have to be illuminated while the building is occupied. This illumination has to be at least 1 foot candle at floor level. The illumination should be powered by the same electrical supply as the rest of the building. However, there must be an emergency electrical system to illuminate important areas in the event of a power failure. A power system should be able to run for at least 90 minutes, and should be powered by batteries, unit equipment, or a generator. This emergency system should provide at least 1 foot candle average illumination at floor level. Some diminution of illumination is allowed towards the end of the run cycle.

Emergency lighting system

The state of California has outlined specific guidelines for the performance of emergency lighting systems. It is acceptable for these systems to be powered by the normal energy source, so long as there is an alternate source of power (e.g., a generator or batteries) in the event of emergencies. When there is a blackout, a means of egress must be illuminated by an emergency electrical system. The system

- 22 -

Copyright © Mometrix Media. You have been licensed one copy of this document for personal use only. Any other reproduction or redistribution is strictly prohibited. All rights reserved.

must illuminate the following areas in buildings with two or more means of egress: hallways and exit passageways, aisles and unenclosed egress stairways, exterior egress components not at the level of exit discharge, appropriate interior exit discharge elements, and exterior landings.

Exit requirements

Building codes and regulations mandate a certain number of exits in various kinds and sizes of structures. Every building is required to have at least one exit. The occupancy and the occupant load of a space are the two main factors that determine whether a space requires two exits. If the occupant load is between 501 and 1000, a space is required to have more than two exits. A space may also be required to supply additional exits if the distance from a given spot in the space to the nearest exit is above a certain amount. This distance is known as the common path of egress travel.

Building codes mandate the arrangement and width of exits in commercial and other public buildings. In a room that needs two exits, the exits must be at least half the diagonal distance of the building or space they serve. For a space that has been equipped with sprinklers and which requires two exits, the minimum separation between them is one-third the diagonal distance of the space. Minimum exit width is calculated by multiplying the occupant load by the appropriate factor given in the building code. There are also strict maximum travel distances for buildings of various sizes and configurations. The maximum travel distance is the greatest distance from any point in a building to the entrance of the nearest exit.

Copyright © Mometrix Media. You have been licensed one copy of this document for personal use only. Any other reproduction or redistribution is strictly prohibited. All rights reserved.

Accessibility

Corridor requirements

The Americans with Disabilities Act has established strict standards for corridors. At the very least, a corridor has to be 36 inches across (32 inches at a doorway). When the occupant load is greater than 50, the corridor must be at least 44 inches wide. A corridor is allowed to have a slope of up to 1:20. In a means of egress system, exit access areas are those areas that do not have a protected path of travel and which lead to the entrance of an exit. The International Building Code of 2006 includes fire-rated corridors in this category.

Door requirements

The Americans with Disabilities Act has established strict standards for doors. Door handles must be easy to grasp, meaning that standard doorknobs are usually not allowed. Door closers, where they exist, must be adjusted to be slow enough to allow handicapped individuals to enter and exit. The opening force of an automatic door must not exceed 5 pounds per foot. A fully opened door may only project into a hallway a maximum of 7 inches. The minimum clear width of an exit door is 32 inches. A door threshold cannot be more than a half-inch in height and has to be beveled such that a wheelchair can get over it easily.

Doorway requirements

The Americans with Disabilities Act has established strict standards for doorways. It asserts that doorways must have a minimum clear opening width of 32 inches and a maximum depth of 24 inches. Thresholds cannot exceed one-half inch in height and must be leveled so that the slope is never greater than 1:2. There are specific clearances that are mandated so that a latch can be undone and the door can be swung open without blocking the adjacent rooms or corridors. Doors must have handles than can be manipulated easily, and door closers must contribute to easing the closing of the door.

Stairway requirements

The Americans with Disabilities Act has established strict standards for stairways. The maximum height of a stair riser is 7 inches in commercial construction, while the minimum depth of a stair tread in commercial construction is 11 inches. There must be continuous stair rails on both sides of a stairway. The risers cannot be open in a public building, and the selection of nosing styles is strictly delimited. An area of refuge is a place in a building where those people who cannot use stairways can wait for assistance during an emergency evacuation.

Copyright © Mometrix Media. You have been licensed one copy of this document for personal use only. Any other reproduction or redistribution is strictly prohibited. All rights reserved.

Residential exiting requirements

The International Building Code has established strict standards for residential exiting. Exit corridors must be at least 36 inches wide and are allowed to pass through kitchens and bathrooms. It must be possible to open every lock in the residence from the inside. Basements and second stories only need to have one exit. Every basement and bedroom is required to have an access window that opens to a height of at least 24 inches. It is permissible for doors to open into rooms, since the low occupant load in a residence indicates that this will not block passageways in any significant way.

Accessible route requirements

The Americans with Disabilities Act has established strict standards for accessible routes. Accessible routes must be designed so that they can be used by individuals in wheelchairs. To this end, the minimum clear width must be 36 inches throughout and at least 32 inches at doorways. Doorways and passages cannot be more than 24 inches across. The minimum passage width for two wheelchairs is 60 inches. If the accessible route is below 60 inches in width, then passing spaces of at least 60" x 60" must be provided at intervals no greater than 200 feet. The minimum clear floor space for a stationary wheelchair is 30" x 48". An accessible route may have a slope of as much as 1:20, but if it is any greater a ramp is required.

Plumbing fixture and drinking fountain requirements

The Americans with Disabilities Act has established strict standards for plumbing fixtures and drinking fountains. Plumbing fixtures include drinking fountains, bathtubs, showers, urinals, sinks, and lavatories. Every toilet room must have a turning space of five square feet in order to accommodate wheelchairs. Public spaces are required to provide separate drinking fountains for wheelchair-bound and standing individuals. A drinking fountain must have a clear space of 30" x 48" available for front approach. If the drinking fountain stands freely or is built into a wall without clear space underneath, there must be 30" x 48" in front to allow a parallel approach.

Toilet stall requirements

The Americans with Disabilities Act (ADA) has established strict standards for toilet stalls. It mandates that toilet rooms must have a minimum clear circular turning space of 5 feet. It is allowed, however, for the clear floor space and space for fixtures and controls to overlap with the turning space. According to the ADA, the amount of clearance depth required for a toilet depends on whether the toilet is hung on the wall or mounted on the floor. In general, the door to the stall must provide a minimum clear opening of 32 inches and must swing away from the stall enclosure. Grab bars must be mounted at between 33 and 36 inches above the floor. The

Copyright © Mometrix Media. You have been licensed one copy of this document for personal use only. Any other reproduction or redistribution is strictly prohibited. All rights reserved.

centerline of the toilet must be 18 inches from a wall with grab bars at both the back and side of the closet.

Urinals and lavatory requirements

The Americans with Disabilities Act (ADA) has established strict standards for urinals, lavatories, and drinking fountains. According to the ADA, urinals must be either of the stall type or must be hung on the wall with an elongated rim at a maximum height of 17 inches above the floor. There must be 30" x 48" of clear floor space in front of the urinal. A lavatory must allow access for a person in a wheelchair to move under the sink and easily use the water controls with one hand. All pipes must be insulated or otherwise blocked from human contact. All mirrors must be mounted with the bottom edge of the reflecting surface at a maximum height of 40 inches above the floor.

Bathtub and shower requirements

The Americans with Disabilities Act has established strict standards for bathtubs and showers. A bathtub or shower must have a seat. In a bathtub, any provided enclosure cannot obstruct the controls or obstruct transfer from the wheelchair to the seat or into the tub. The tracks on which the enclosure rests cannot be mounted on the rim of the tub. There are a couple of acceptable configurations for showers, one of which requires a permanent seat, while the other only requires a fold-out seat. Grab bars in a shower or bathtub must be provided between 33 and 36 inches above the floor.

Floor surface requirements

The Americans with Disabilities Act has established strict standards for floor surfaces. The maximum allowable vertical change in floor level for an accessible floor is one fourth of an inch. The maximum allowable slope for an accessible ramp is one vertical unit for every 12 force on all units (8.33%). According to the Americans with Disabilities Act, all floor surfaces must be stable, hard and resistant to slipping. If there is carpet, the pile height can be no greater than one-half inch. When there are changes in the height of the floor surface of less than one-quarter inch, no edge treatment is required (that is, the transition can be vertical). If the change in floor surface is between one-quarter inch and one-half inch, the transition must be beveled with a slope no greater than 1:2. If the change in floor surface is greater than one-half inch, a suitable transition and a ramp are required.

Ramp requirements

The Americans with Disabilities Act (ADA) has established strict standards for ramps. The ADA mandates that ramps may have a slope no greater than 1:12. The maximum rise of any ramp is 30 inches. Any change in elevation greater than 30 inches requires a level landing before the next round of ramp. The minimum clear

Copyright © Mometrix Media. You have been licensed one copy of this document for personal use only. Any other reproduction or redistribution is strictly prohibited. All rights reserved.

width for a ramp is 36 inches and the minimum landing length is either 60 inches or an amount equal to the widest ramp intersecting the landing. If the landing changes directions, it must be at least 60 inches square. Any ramp with a rise greater than 6 inches or a length greater than 72 inches must have handrails on both sides. The top of the handrail must be between 34 to 38 inches above the ramp, and the handrails must extend at least a foot beyond the ends of the ramp. The handrail must have a diameter of between 1 1/4 inches and 1 1/2 inches.

Stair handrail requirements

The Americans with Disabilities Act (ADA) has established strict standards for handrails on stairs. The handrail on an accessible stairway must extend beyond the upper and lower risers. The ADA mandates that handrails must be continuous on each side of a set of stairs. The top of the handrail must be between 34 and 38 inches above the stair nosing and must extend a minimum of 1 foot beyond the ends of the stairs. There must be 1 1/4 inch to 1 1/2 inch of clear space between the handrail and the wall. When an exit stairway is part of an accessible route in a building without sprinklers, there must be 4 feet of clear width between the handrails.

Protruding object requirements

The Americans with Disabilities Act (ADA) sets specific guidelines for the presence of protruding objects, which can be a particular hazard for visually impaired individuals. A protruding object with a lower edge less than 27 inches above the floor is assumed to be detectable with a cane and therefore may protrude any amount. A protruding object may not reduce the clear width required for an accessible route or maneuvering space. If the vertical clearance of an area adjacent to an accessible route is reduced to less than 80 inches, a guardrail or other barrier must be provided.

Detectable warning requirements

The Americans with Disabilities Act (ADA) has established specific guidelines for detectable warnings, so that handicapped individuals will be able to ascertain hazardous situations. The walking surfaces in front of stairs, hazardous vehicle areas, or any other hazardous locations must have detectable warning surfaces unless there is a guardrail or some other method of warning. The texture of a detectable warning surface must contrast with the surrounding surface. Doors which lead to potentially dangerous areas must have different textures than normal doors in the building. Detectable warnings are required on walking surfaces in front of hazardous vehicular areas.

Signage requirements

The Americans with Disabilities Act (ADA) has established strict standards for signage. The international symbol for accessibility must be placed on parking

Copyright © Mometrix Media. You have been licensed one copy of this document for personal use only. Any other reproduction or redistribution is strictly prohibited. All rights reserved.

spaces, passenger loading zones, accessible entrances and toilet and bathing facilities. According to the ADA, all permanent rooms and spaces must be identified. The lettering of a sign must be between 5/8 inch and 2 inches high and must be raised 1/32 inch above the surface of the sign. The letters must be in all uppercase in a sans serif or simple serif font and must be accompanied by grade 2 Braille. Any pictograms must be at least 6 inches high and must be accompanied by verbal descriptions.

Permanent identification signs must have an egg shell matte or other glare-resistant finish and must be composed such that characters and symbols contrast with the background. They must be mounted on the wall adjacent to the latch side of the door and must be approachable to within 3 inches without encountering protruding objects or standing within the swing of the door. The distance from the mounting height to the centerline of the sign must be 60 inches. In situations where there is no wall space on the left side of the door, the sign should be placed on the nearest adjacent wall. Directional signs must have lettering a minimum of 3 inches high with a width-to-height ratio from 3:5 to 1:1. The contrast and finish requirements for directional signs are the same as those for permanent room identification signs.

Alarm requirements

The Americans with Disabilities Act Accessibility Guidelines (ADAAG) mandate that alarms should be audible and visible. The ADAAG has established that the maximum vertical reach dimension for accessibility is 48 inches. Emergency warning systems must provide both a visual and audible alarm. An audible alarm must exceed the usual sound level in the room by at least 15 dB. A visual alarm must be composed of flashing lights with a frequency of approximately 1 cycle per second. The general rule for alarms is that they must be immediately recognizable to visually and hearing-impaired individuals. Interior designers can consult with emergency alarm specialists to determine the appropriate alarm system for a given project.

Public telephone requirements

The Americans with Disabilities Act has placed restrictions on the types and arrangements of phones that can be made available in a public setting. In situations where public telephones are provided, at least one of the telephones must comply with the requirements of the Americans with Disabilities Act. When there are two or more banks of telephones, at least one telephone at each bank must comply with these requirements. If there are four or more public pay telephones, at least one of the interior public telephones must be a text telephone.

Elevator requirements

The Americans with Disabilities Act has established strict standards for elevators. The call buttons on an elevator must indicate when the call is received and responded to. Hall lanterns must give visual and audible signals. It is typical for the

Copyright © Mometrix Media. You have been licensed one copy of this document for personal use only. Any other reproduction or redistribution is strictly prohibited. All rights reserved.

lantern to chime once for up and twice for down. The floor buttons on the inside of the car may be no higher than 54 inches above the floor. Moreover, the emergency controls must be no more than 35 inches above the ground and must be in the center of the button display.

Copyright © Mometrix Media. You have been licensed one copy of this document for personal use only. Any other reproduction or redistribution is strictly prohibited. All rights reserved.

Building Systems

Water conservation restrictions

The state of California encourages the use of low-flow toilets and urinals. It is generally recommended that toilets consume a maximum of 1.6 gallons of water with each flush. Urinals, on the other hand, should consume no more than 1 gallon per flush. In public restrooms, metered faucets should deliver no more than a quarter gallon of water per cycle. There are no restrictions on the amount of water used by an emergency safety shower. California also encourages the use of low-flow showerheads. The state asserts that the use of such a fixture in combination with a faucet aerator (which adds air to the water stream) saves an average of 7800 gallons of water annually.

Electrical conductors

An interior designer needs to be familiar with the basic electrical conductors. Electrical conductors are the wires that connect the circuit breaker to the various electrical appliances in a building. A nonmetallic sheathed cable (Romex) is composed of multiple plastic insulated conductors and a ground wire covered by a plastic jacket. These cables can be used in buildings three stories or less. A flexible metal clad cable, also known as armored cable or flex cable, is composed of multiple plastic insulated conductors with a surrounding continuous strip of steel tape. These cables are used on commercial light fixtures and in remodeling work. Under-carpet wiring is flat and insulated wiring. Grounding wires are supplied in addition to those that conduct electricity so that if somebody accidentally touches a short-circuited appliance they will not be electrocuted. A ground fault interrupter finds any minute current leaks and immediately halts the power being delivered to a circuit.

Residential electrical outlet requirements

In the state of California, electrical sockets must be present on any wall that is greater than two feet wide. There cannot be a space of more than 12 feet separating two sockets on a wall. These rules apply to living rooms, bedrooms, and kitchen walls. Along kitchen countertops, there must be an outlet along any counter surface wider than one foot, and there cannot be spaces of more than four feet in between outlets. In the kitchen, electrical outlets must have two circuits of 20 amps and 125 volts. In the dining room, living room, and bedroom, outlets also are usually at 20 amps, 125 volts.

Ground fault circuit interrupters

In California, ground fault circuit interrupters are used to reduce the risk of electric shock. These devices, sometimes referred to as GFCIs, are affixed to the main

Copyright © Mometrix Media. You have been licensed one copy of this document for personal use only. Any other reproduction or redistribution is strictly prohibited. All rights reserved.

electrical panel, from which they can provide safety to all the outlets served by that box. When there is a large surge of electricity, the ground fault circuit interrupter can break the circuit. This prevents people from receiving an electric shock from coming into contact with the outlet. For instance, if a person is standing in water, touching an outlet may allow the electricity to flow through the person's body creating a serious shock. The GFCI can recognize this rapid change in voltage and cut off the circuit.

Plumbing hardware

An interior designer needs to be familiar with the common hardware used in plumbing. For instance, a stack vent connects to a soil or waste stack above the highest fixture. A stack is simply a vertical pipe. A vent stack is a pipe distinct from a soil or waste stack. A soil stack carries human waste. A waste stack carries all other forms of waste besides human waste. A plumbing trap holds a certain amount of water, thus forming a seal that prevents gas from the sewage system from entering the atmosphere of the building.

Lighting fixture labels

An interior decorator can obtain useful information from the labels on lighting fixtures. Three of the most common labels in the state of California are ENERGY STAR, Title 24, and Airtight:

ENERGY STAR indicates that the fixture meets a minimum standard of efficiency and quality. All of these fixtures are compliant with Title 24.

Title 24 indicates that a fixture meets the performance standards established in 2005 with the revision of Title 24.

Airtight is only required for recessed fixtures that have been installed in an insulated space. Sometimes, this label will read ASTM E283, indicating that the fixture has passed a particular laboratory test of airtightness.

Lighting efficiency technologies

There are three lighting technologies that are practically guaranteed to comply with Title 24: high-efficacy luminaires, sensors, and dimmers. High-efficacy luminaires are only capable of operating light sources that are energy efficient. For instance, high-efficacy luminaires are used in high-intensity discharge lamps, compact fluorescent lamps, and fluorescent T8 lamps. Sensors, meanwhile, are devices that automatically turn off lights when certain conditions are met. For example, many new houses have motion sensors that only turn on outside lighting when movement is detected. Finally, a dimmer is a device that allows the occupants of a space to lower the lights to their satisfaction.

Copyright © Mometrix Media. You have been licensed one copy of this document for personal use only. Any other reproduction or redistribution is strictly prohibited. All rights reserved.

High-efficacy luminaires

Interior designers need to know the general standards for high-efficacy luminaires, so that they can be sure to comply with Title 24. The required efficacy of a lamp depends upon the lamp's power. So, for instance, a lamp with power of less than 15 watts need only have an efficacy of 40 lumens per watt. A lamp with power of 15 to 40 watts, however, must have efficacy of at least 50 lumens per watt. When the lamp has greater than 40 watts of power, the required lamp efficacy is 60 lumens per watt. The ENERGY STAR program has made it considerably easier for decorators to identify high-efficacy luminaires; all of the fixtures that bear this label meet the standards of Title 24. The two most common types are fixtures with HID lamps and fluorescent and CFL fixtures with electronic ballasts.

As a designer, the choice of lighting fixtures is only somewhat limited by Title 24. There are still some important choices to make. For instance, fluorescent bulbs come in a range of colors, most of which are variations on white. In most residential situations, a warmer bulb is preferred. The warmer fluorescent bulbs more closely approximate incandescent lighting. In situations where fluorescent bulbs are replacing incandescent bulbs, it may be necessary to adjust the total number of fixtures. As for ballast, most interior designers prefer the more common electronic ballasts, which tend to flicker less than bulbs with magnetic ballast. Finally, a designer should always opt for thermally managed fixtures where possible, since these reduce the danger of overheating.

Energy usage sensors

Many interior designers incorporate sensors into their lighting plan as a means of minimizing energy usage. Sensors turn lights off or on according to stimuli in the environment. For instance, there are sensors that will automatically turn off the lights in a room when it is empty. In the interest of efficacy, sensors that automatically turn on when a person enters the room are not allowed, unless the lights were turned off in the last thirty seconds (these are useful when a person has been motionless but has not left the room). In order to be compliant with the state of California regulations, a sensor must turn on manually and turn off automatically, though sensors are allowed to turn off manually as well. A sensor should not have a time delay of more than thirty minutes, and should not be capable of being locked in the on position. Finally, any sensors used outside should have a photocell that prevents them from turning on during the day.

Occupancy and vacancy sensors

When using occupancy and vacancy sensors in a lighting system, interior designers should consider whether the sensor is able to comprehensively survey the area in question. In other words, there should not be any obstructions to a sensor. Most interior designers find that sensors are most appropriate for laundry rooms, utility closets, bathrooms, and garages. Inexperienced decorators should stay away from

Copyright © Mometrix Media. You have been licensed one copy of this document for personal use only. Any other reproduction or redistribution is strictly prohibited. All rights reserved.

wall box occupancy sensors in three-way applications, as these have a tendency towards confusion. Finally, the designer should make sure that the electrical load requirements of the sensor are being met. If the minimum load rating of the sensor is significantly more than the power of the lighting source, the sensor may not work.

Dimmers

Dimmers are devices that allow occupants to raise or lower lights to their satisfaction. These switches are often less expensive than high-efficacy luminaires or sensors. There are a number of different types of dimmer switch, including models designed for low voltage, line voltage, and three-way applications. Some dimmers have both a slide or knob and an on/off switch, which allows the user to turn lights all the way off immediately. The range of loads to be managed by the dimmer switch should be considered ahead of time, because not all dimmers are capable of managing heavy loads.

Interior designers love dimmers because they are a cheap way to comply with Title 24 standards. However, there are a few important considerations related to the use of these devices. For instance, a dimmer designed for standard incandescent lighting may not work with a high-efficacy or fluorescent luminaire. Fluorescent luminaires require special ballasts and dimmers in order to be raised or lowered by degree. When the dimmer is not properly matched with the electrical lighting load of the fixtures, one of the components in the lighting system may be stressed and fail. The dimming of low-voltage fixtures may require the addition of components to prevent the dimmer from overheating. Ultimately, most designers find that the best rooms for dimmers are living rooms, bedrooms, and dining rooms.

Kitchen lighting

A kitchen is defined as any room used for the preparation, cooking, or storage of food. If an adjacent area is lit with the same switches as the kitchen, it is considered part of the kitchen. In the state of California, up to half of the total wattage used in a kitchen can be low efficacy. However, the state encourages designers to incorporate a greater proportion of high-efficacy lighting. Regardless of the proportion, all of the high-efficacy lighting must be controlled by different switches than the low-efficacy lighting. However, the 2005 standards eliminated the switch location requirement of the past.

The California Energy Code outlines specific rules related to kitchen lighting. At least half of the permanently installed lighting must be high efficacy. Most of the time, this sort of lighting will be fluorescent. All of the lighting fixtures on the ceiling or the wall are considered permanent, though other fixtures may be considered permanent as well. Each of these fixtures is counted as part of the total wattage, and therefore must comply with state standards. The occupant should be able to turn off at least half of the lighting in the room without losing illumination of the entire

Copyright © Mometrix Media. You have been licensed one copy of this document for personal use only. Any other reproduction or redistribution is strictly prohibited. All rights reserved.

room. In other words, turning off half of the lighting should not create areas of excessive darkness.

According to the Energy Code of the state of California, there must be separate controls for fluorescent and incandescent fixtures. In the past, California required that the first switch operate a fluorescent light fixture. This is no longer the case. There is no required amount of fixtures in a kitchen, as the appropriate number will vary according to the size and configuration of the space. If the interior designer wants nook lighting to be counted separately than the rest of the kitchen, the nook lighting must be on a different switch and comply with efficacy standards. Finally, when fixtures are amenable to different lamp wattages, the wattage is defined as the highest designated by the manufacturer on the UL label.

Bathroom lighting

The state of California has outlined specific standards related to bathroom lighting. A bathroom is defined as any room containing a tub, shower, toilet, or sink to be used for personal hygiene. The lighting system in a bathroom must either be high-efficacy or must be operated by an occupancy sensor that is turned on manually. If there are incandescent and fluorescent fixtures in the same bathroom, these distinct fixtures should be operated with separate switches. In the past, it was necessary for the first switch to control a fluorescent fixture; this regulation is no longer in place. Any occupancy sensors must turn on manually but off automatically. At the very most, sensors can turn off thirty minutes after the last detected motion. Moreover, it is not permitted to have a sensor that is capable of keeping the light fixture on permanently.

The state of California Energy Code mandates that every single permanent fixture in a bathroom must comply with standards. In other words, every fixture must be either high efficacy or operated by an occupancy sensor that can only turn on manually. However, there is no particular requirement related to the number of light fixtures. This is because the need for light fixtures will depend on the size and layout of the bathroom. In general, interior designers prefer fluorescent light fixtures with manual switches, since these will not go off while the occupant lies motionless in a bath. Also, it is a good idea to use the 26-watt CFL recessed cans commonly used in the kitchen, since this similarity will make it easy for the occupant to buy replacement parts.

Bedroom lighting

The California Energy Code states that all interior rooms besides kitchens and bathrooms must have high-efficacy lighting, manual-on occupancy sensors, or dimmer switch. Every permanent lighting fixture in a bedroom, for instance, must meet one of these three conditions. In a bedroom, it is a good idea to use two different switches for the fan and lights of a ceiling fan. Typically, interior designers opt for either fluorescent fixtures with one or more regular switches or

Copyright © Mometrix Media. You have been licensed one copy of this document for personal use only. Any other reproduction or redistribution is strictly prohibited. All rights reserved.

incandescent fixtures with occupancy sensors or dimmers. There do not need to be special controls for switched outlets in a bedroom. Also, it is considered proper to leave two switch wires when installing a switched ceiling box without a fixture, so that the occupant can install a ceiling fan with light fixture later on.

Entry, foyer, and hallway lighting

The California Energy Code declares that entry areas, foyers, and hallways must be lit by high-efficacy luminaires or must have dimmer switches or occupancy sensors that turn on manually. This means that every permanent fixture in one of these areas must meet one of those three conditions. There are two common approaches to lighting these transitional areas. One is to use fluorescent light fixtures with regular three-way switching. The other is to use incandescent fixtures outfitted with three-way dimmers. An interior designer can use line voltage dimmers, low-voltage dimmers with magnetic transformers, or low-voltage dimmers with electronic transformers.

Living room lighting

The Energy Code places living rooms in the same category as all other interior rooms besides bathrooms and kitchens, meaning that all permanent fixtures must be high efficacy, operated by a dimmer switch, or operated by an occupancy sensor that turns on manually. In living rooms, interior designers tend to opt for incandescent fixtures with dimmers or fluorescent fixtures with one or more regular switches. If the living room has a ceiling fan with a light, there should be different regular switches for each of these functions. If the ceiling fan has an incandescent light kit, there should be a regular switch for the fan and a dimmer switch for the light. Finally, switched outlets do not require special controls.

Dining room, enclosed patio, and attic lighting

Dining rooms, enclosed patios, and attics must be outfitted with high-efficacy luminaires, occupancy sensors that turn on manually, or dimmer switches. In a dining room, many interior designers prefer to combine incandescent fixtures with dimmer switches, since these provide a more ambient and warm atmosphere. Despite being only semi-finished, enclosed patios and attics are subject to the same lighting restrictions as all rooms besides bathrooms and kitchens. When an attic is controlled by a normal switch, it makes sense to use fluorescent lighting. The use of occupancy sensors in attics is discouraged unless the sensor can easily observe the entirety of the space.

HVAC system

The following HVAC considerations must be made during any construction process: space for ducts, pipes, and mixing boxes; plenum requirements; access; thermostats; coordination with other ceiling items; window coverings; space planning and

Copyright © Mometrix Media. You have been licensed one copy of this document for personal use only. Any other reproduction or redistribution is strictly prohibited. All rights reserved.

furniture placement; and acoustic separation. The space between the suspended ceiling and the structural floor above it is called the plenum. A convector is a coil unit used to heat water. A mixing box mitigates noise, slows air, and makes fine adjustments to the temperature or quantity of the air going into a particular space. A sole plate is a horizontal wood member that functions as a base for the studs in a wood-stud partition. A toilet carrier is a framework made of steel and bolted to the floor to support the weight of a toilet hung on the wall. A chase wall is composed of two runs of studs divided by however much space is needed to accommodate pipes. An access door allows entry to the mechanical and electrical components between walls. It is usually made out of steel and opened with a thumb turn or key.

Copyright © Mometrix Media. You have been licensed one copy of this document for personal use only. Any other reproduction or redistribution is strictly prohibited. All rights reserved.

Miscellaneous

Interior glazing

Interior designers should be familiar with the following types of interior glazing:

- Float glass (also known as annealed glass): The most common form of glass used in windows. It does not provide a great degree of strength, so it is not appropriate for providing extra safety or security.

- Tempered glass: Regular float glass that has been hardened through a special heat process. The resulting tempered glass is approximately four times as strong as regular glass and breaks into tiny, rounded pieces rather than sharp shards.

- Laminated glass: Both tempered glass and laminated glass can be used as glazing in hazardous locations, so long as they pass test 16 CFR 1201, Category II.

- Wire glass: A pane of glass with a sheet of wire embedded in its center. The wire keeps the glass from shattering when broken and prohibits forcible entry into a building.

- Patterned glass: Regular glass which has been passed through a roller in order to embed a pattern. Virtually any pattern can be applied to glass, with variable degrees of opacity resulting. It is also possible to pattern a piece of glass so that some parts of the pane are more transparent than others.

- Fire-rated glazing: Can be divided into four subcategories: ceramic with a high impact resistance and low expansion coefficient, tempered fire-protective glass, several layers of fire-protected glass separated by a transparent polymer gel, and rated glass block.

- Electrochromic glazing: Cannot become totally opaque. It is created with an inorganic ceramic film that coats the outside surface of the pane.

- SPD glazing: Microscopic particles are spread throughout a film that runs between two panes of glass. It is capable of becoming totally opaque and can be controlled with a rheostat.

- Polymer-dispersed liquid crystal film glazing: A film is placed in between two pieces of glass. It cannot become totally opaque.

Copyright © Mometrix Media. You have been licensed one copy of this document for personal use only. Any other reproduction or redistribution is strictly prohibited. All rights reserved.

Professional Ethics

CID code of ethics and conduct

The California Council for Interior Design Certification was established in 1992 to standardize the education and professional practice of interior designers. This organization also aims to protect the public by enforcing compliance with its Code of Ethics and Conduct. The Council for Interior Design Code of Ethics and Conduct mandates that interior designers perform their duties in such a manner as to win the admiration of the general public and of colleagues in the industry. The CCIDC expects all interior design professionals to abide by the standards laid out in the Code. The Code is divided into five subcategories. In the first, the object of the Code is discussed. The remaining four subcategories describe the interior designer's responsibilities to the public, the client, other certified interior designers and colleagues, and the profession in general.

CID's responsibility to the public

The CID Code of Ethics and Conduct defines the responsibilities of a Certified Interior Designer to the public. To begin with, a CID must follow all of the laws and regulations that apply to his or her work, and must always act with what the law considers to be reasonable care and competence. At times, this means putting the health, safety, and welfare of the public first. A CID cannot break the law, and cannot encourage or influence a client or colleague to do so. A CID is not allowed to accept payment for services he or she is not authorized to provide. For instance, a CID cannot be paid for construction or installation unless he or she has the right contractor's license. Also, a CID should not affix his or her name or signature to work which he or she did not perform or direct.

The CID Code of Ethics and Conduct asserts that Certified Interior Designers should not engage in misleading or false advertising, and should ensure that their employees do not do so either. Also, CIDs should be careful to avoid implying that employees are certified unless they are so. In general, CIDs are prohibited from making false or misleading claims about their professional practice. A CID should not engage in any behavior which could be construed as fraudulent, deceptive, or dishonest. A CID must not discriminate on the basis of national origin, race, religion, gender, sexual orientation, age, or non-disqualifying handicap. A CID should not accede to any request made by a superior, which would require the CID to violate any laws, regulations, or items in the Code.

CID's responsibility to the client

The CID Code of Ethics and Conduct outlines the responsibilities of a Certified Interior Designer to his or her client. A CID should only agree to perform those

Copyright © Mometrix Media. You have been licensed one copy of this document for personal use only. Any other reproduction or redistribution is strictly prohibited. All rights reserved.

services for which he or she has been trained and for which he or she is qualified. A CID should give the client an idea of the scope and duration of the project before beginning work. A CID should also settle the methods to be used as well as the protocol for payment. There should not be any changes to this plan unless they are agreed to by the client. A CID should have the client sign a detailed, comprehensive contract before work begins. This contract should include a description of the services to be performed, the method of payment, the schedule for payment, and the system of legal remedy (for instance, arbitration).

If a CID has a financial interest that could potentially conflict with the completion of a contract, he or she must notify the client immediately and in writing. Potential conflicts of interest include any affiliations that would influence the CID's selection of materials or contractors. The client should be given the option to terminate the contract if he or she cannot accept the conflict of interest. A CID is bound by strict confidentiality requirements. A CID is not allowed to disclose any information about a client, a client's intentions, or a client's productions methods, so long as the client has requested confidentiality or the disclosure could conceivably affect the interests of the client in an adverse manner. However, a CID is required to disclose information about the client when it is necessary to preserve the safety of the public or to prevent a violation of the law.

CID's responsibility to other CIDs and colleagues

The CID Code of Ethics and Conduct outlines the responsibilities of a Certified Interior Designers to other CIDs and colleagues. In general, CIDs are required to act honestly and fairly, and to demonstrate respect for the professional relationships of colleagues and other CIDs. A CID is forbidden from participating in any activity or conversation that might cause unjust damage to the professional practice of another CID or colleague. A CID is not allowed to plagiarize the work of other professionals, and is not allowed to accept work from clients that has been plagiarized from other interior design professionals. A CID is not allowed to recommend another professional who he or she knows to be unqualified in terms of education, training, or character. A CID should never misrepresent the work of another professional, and should never take credit for work that was performed by another professional.

CID's responsibility to the profession

The CID Code of Ethics and Conduct outlines the duties of a Certified Interior Designer to the profession in general. A CID is required to abide by the highest professional and personal standards. He or she should always be seeking ways to improve his or her professional practice, whether through continuing education or mentorship programs. A CID should communicate with other CIDs and interior design professionals, and should contribute to the transmission of information throughout the industry. Finally, CIDs are forbidden from making false or misleading statements or failing to disclose important information related to certification or renewal of certification.

Copyright © Mometrix Media. You have been licensed one copy of this document for personal use only. Any other reproduction or redistribution is strictly prohibited. All rights reserved.

Legal Issues

Business, tax, and professional licensure requirements

Like any other business, an interior design firm needs to acquire a business license in the relevant jurisdiction so that it can be monitored and taxed. A sales tax license (resale license) gives the interior designer the ability to buy furniture at wholesale and sell it at retail. In addition, some states require that an interior designer have some form of professional licensure in order to practice. Businesses that have employees must withhold state and federal taxes as per tax law and must obtain an employer identification number from the Internal Revenue Service.

Agency, duties, and liability

There are a few legal issues with which an interior designer should be familiar before beginning practice. Agency is the legal term that describes the relationship in which the designer acts on behalf of the client when meeting and making transactions with a contractor or vendor. An agent is defined as any person who is given the responsibility to act on behalf of another person. The duties of an interior designer are stated in the terms of the contract, are established in the laws of the jurisdiction of practice and are implied by the scenario in which the business arrangement is made. Liabilities are all of the obligations an interior designer incurs during the course of business. All of these obligations must be fulfilled with currency, goods, or services.

Negligence, risk management, exposure to third party claims, and copyright

An interior designer should be familiar with a few legal issues before beginning practice. Negligence is any behavior which puts another person in danger, either directly or indirectly. An interior designer is considered negligent anytime he or she fails to fulfill the implied or stated duties of his or her position. Risk management is a systematic approach to analyzing the presence of risk and selecting and implementing protective techniques. Interior designers need to minimize risk whenever possible. Interior designers should also take steps to avoid exposure to third-party claims. This is mainly done through indemnification clauses and through maintaining good communication with contractors and employees. Finally, copyright is the legal right given to a creator to produce and distribute his or her creation exclusively.

Certified interior designers

The state of California has outlined specific definitions for certified interior designers and interior design organizations. These are given in the Business and

Copyright © Mometrix Media. You have been licensed one copy of this document for personal use only. Any other reproduction or redistribution is strictly prohibited. All rights reserved.

Professions Code, Chapter 3.9, Section 5800. A certified interior designer is any person who creates and issues plans to a building department, so long as those plans are of sufficient complexity to merit completion by a licensed contractor. A certified contractor is also a person who programs, plans, designs, and documents the construction and installation of interior design elements. A certified interior designer must have attained a level of competency through education, experience, or the passage of an examination.

Interior design organizations

According to the state of California, an interior design organization is any nonprofit group of certified interior designers that has a governing board which includes representatives of the public. Interior design organizations, as nonprofit entities, are exempt from taxation under Section 501(c)(3) of Title 26 of the United States Code. So long as the paperwork has been submitted to the Internal Revenue Service in a reasonable interval, any organizations that are not yet exempt from taxation under that code can still be designated in California as an interior design organization.

Seller's permit, and sales tax

Interior designers only need a seller's permit when they sell merchandise directly to clients. For instance, some interior designers sell samples or finished drawings to clients. For this transaction, a seller's permit is required. A seller's permit is also required for sales of furniture, window coverings, carpeting, cabinets, and other home accessories. When this sort of merchandise is sold, the interior designer probably needs to pay the sales tax. The sales tax is based on the retail selling price of the merchandise, including markup and related service and labor charges. If the item is attached to real property, however, it may count as an improvement to real property and therefore be covered by a different standard.

Taxation

In the state of California, an interior designer must charge sales tax on fees for professional service when those fees are directly related to a taxable sale of merchandise. However, the interior designer does not have to apply sales tax when the fees for professional service are not related to the sale of merchandise. Similarly, sales tax must be applied on labor charges related to fabrication labor, but need not be applied to repair or installation labor, or to labor performed on real property. A sales tax must be applied to the sale of merchandise when the interior designer is the retailer of the merchandise.

The services typically performed by an interior designer are consulting, design, layout, coordination of furniture and fabrics, installation supervision, and project management. The fee assessed by an interior design professional does not have to be negotiated fixed amount. It can also be a percentage of the selling price of the furnishings, labor, and installation charges. All of the fees that are directly related to

Copyright © Mometrix Media. You have been licensed one copy of this document for personal use only. Any other reproduction or redistribution is strictly prohibited. All rights reserved.

the acquisition and provision of furnishings and other merchandise that are sold to a client need to be taxed. All of the fees that are not related to the sale of merchandise are not taxable.

If labor is associated with a taxable sale, labor charges may be taxed. There are three types of labor charge: those related to fabrication, repair, and installation. The first type is generally taxable, while the latter two are not. Repair and installation labor charges therefore need to be itemized separately on the invoice. Fabrication labor is related to the creation of new items or the alteration of existing items, so long as these items are then sold to the client. There are a variety of tasks that count as alteration, including work performed on bedding, garments, draperies, or other household items. Common alterations involve the addition or removal of material, rearranging of the elements, and restyling of the item. Alteration counts as fabrication, and is therefore taxable, regardless of where the materials are obtained.

Repair labor includes the restoration, reconditioning, or refinishing of an object. Some examples of repair labor are relining draperies, refinishing chairs, or cleaning a used carpet. This labor is not taxable so long as the object being repaired is merely being returned to its original use. Installation labor, meanwhile, is necessary to make an object operational once it has been delivered to the client. Installation labor charges are not taxable. However, any equipment or materials that must be purchased in order to perform installation are taxable costs. As an example, plugging in a lamp is an installation cost that requires no extra equipment, and is therefore not taxable.

When an interior decorator subcontracts work, the taxation program is largely the same as when the interior decorator performs the work. That is, when the subcontractor performs fabrication labor, the cost of the item and labor are both taxable. On the other hand, when the subcontractor only performs repair or installation services, the work is not taxable. It is important to obtain a comprehensive list of the materials and labor required by the subcontractor. Many times, subcontractors feel that this is unnecessary because they are not selling directly to the client. However, in order to handle taxation properly, such documentation is essential.

If an interior designer pays for shipping and delivery for nontaxable sales, this cost is not taxable. If the shipping and delivery charges are incurred for a taxable sale, however, the sales are taxable unless four conditions are present. A shipping and delivery charge related to a taxable sale is not taxable if the charges are itemized separately on the invoice, if the delivery is made by a contract or common carrier, if the charges assessed to the client are no more than the charges paid to the carrier, and if the charges are related to transportation directly to the client. All four of these conditions must be met in order for the shipping and delivery charges to not be taxable. Any delivery charges related to transport from the factory or dealer to an intermediate point, as for instance the office of the interior designer, are taxable.

Copyright © Mometrix Media. You have been licensed one copy of this document for personal use only. Any other reproduction or redistribution is strictly prohibited. All rights reserved.

When an interior decorator makes improvements to real property, he or she may be considered a construction contractor for tax purposes. Improvements to real property include furnishing, installing carpet or shutters, or otherwise adding or improving items attached to real property. When these sorts of acts are performed, an interior decorator will be considered a construction contractor for sales and use tax purposes, regardless of whether the decorator is a licensed construction contractor. As a construction contractor, the interior decorator is subject to a different set of rules. It should be noted that interior decorators are not considered contractors when they only supervise the work of a contractor who bills them directly.

In the state of California, there is a different policy for the taxation of fixtures than for the taxation of materials. Fixtures are defined as items or products that do not lose their identity when they are installed. For instance, a set of blinds does not lose its essential character when it is hung in a window. It could be taken down and hung elsewhere in much the same way. Other examples of fixtures include awnings, blinds, heating and air conditioning units, and lighting fixtures. When an interior decorator provides and installs fixtures, the cost of the fixture is taxable, while the cost of installation is not. Materials, on the other hand, are items that lose their identity when they are installed. Paint, for instance, cannot be stripped away and used elsewhere once it has been applied. Other examples of material are carpet, adhesive, and wallpaper. The taxation of materials depends on what has been specified in the construction contract.

Lump-sum vs. time-and-material contracts

There are two general types of construction contract. In a lump-sum contract, all of the charges are assessed as one payment. When this sort of contract is used, the interior decorator is considered the consumer of the materials used to improve the real estate, and therefore does not need to charge the client sales tax on these materials. The cost of the material purchase by the interior decorator is taxable. A use tax is due when the interior decorator does not pay tax at the time of purchase. In a time-and-materials contract, the decorator is considered the consumer so long as he or she does not bill for the materials separately. However, if the client is billed for materials separately and is either assessed sales tax there or is considered the owner of the materials prior to installation, then the interior decorator is considered the retailer and the charge for materials is taxable.

Copyright © Mometrix Media. You have been licensed one copy of this document for personal use only. Any other reproduction or redistribution is strictly prohibited. All rights reserved.

Contractual Issues

Contract elements

An interior designer needs to understand the basic elements of a contract. A contract is defined as an agreement between two or more parties in which each party gives something to the other in return for a desired good or service. By law, there are two parts of a contract: the offer and the acceptance. Although contracts may be written or oral, they must have both an offer and an acceptance in order to be valid. A complete contract includes the parties to the contract and date. This means the full legal name of both parties to the contract, the addresses of both parties, and the date of the contract. All signing individuals must have the authority to give this information.

Every basic contract contains a description of the scope of work and the responsibilities of the designer. The scope of work and designer's responsibilities indicate the precise amount of work promised by the designer, including a detailed description of services. This phase of the contract may be divided into schematic design, design development, and construction phases. Some contracts itemize the services that will not be provided. Purchasing agreements are any arrangements in which the designer is to purchase furniture and fixtures with the consent of the owner. In order to be considered comprehensive, this section of the contract should indicate the designer's responsibility, as well as the client's procedures for payment, acceptance, rejection of damaged goods, installation costs, and methods of purchasing.

Every basic contract contains identification of the method of payment, a summary of reimbursable expenses, and a catalog of extra services. The contract will indicate the amount the client will be charged for services and how payment will be processed (fixed fee, multiple of direct personnel expense, percentage of project costs or cost per unit area). The contract should also indicate when payment is to be made and should include provisions for late payment. Reimbursable expenses are defined as any costs that are not part of professional services, but which have to be endured to complete the project (i.e., travel, utilities, reproduction costs and postage). Occasionally, consultant fees will be included in the section. The extra services outlined in a contract usually include expanding the area of the job or adding more furniture.

A basic contract will outline the responsibilities of the client. These usually include buying and arranging equipment, securing space for the receipt of furniture, providing as-built drawings, and completing on time any work required to allow the services of the designer to continue on schedule. A contract should also indicate the ownership of documents. Typically, the designer will retain the rights of ownership to any documents constructed during the project, so long as they are only used to

Copyright © Mometrix Media. You have been licensed one copy of this document for personal use only. Any other reproduction or redistribution is strictly prohibited. All rights reserved.

complete the specific project for which they were developed. In other words, the client is not allowed to reuse any documents to complete subsequent projects without receiving permission from and compensating the designer. It is typical to place a copyright notice on drawings.

A basic contract contains provisions for arbitration, which outline the procedures for resolving any disputes that should arise during the course of a project. Contracts also include provisions for termination of the contract, which outline the conditions for terminating the contract. Both designer and owner usually have the right to quit the contract as long as adequate written notice is supplied, which is usually a week's notice. When the owner terminates the contract, the client is eligible for compensation if the contract has not been terminated because of any action on his part. Finally, a basic contract, in order to be considered legally valid, needs to be signed by the client, as the designer is assumed to have offered the terms of the contract. Usually, however, both designer and owner sign the contract.

Bid forms

An interior designer may be required to compose a set of instructions to bidders in consultation with the client. The instructions to bidders outline the procedures and requirements bidders must follow during the submission of bids. This set of forms also includes information on how bids will be considered and indicates the submittals that will be required of the successful bidder. The instructions to bidders will also include a listing of all the bonds required by the successful bidder. The owner should be providing advice and requirements to the designer throughout the composition of the bidding documents.

An interior designer may be required to compose a bid form in consultation with the client. The bid form is a standard form on which all bidders enter required information. It is important that all bids be identical in nature, so that the owner and designer will have an easier time comparing them. Typically, it is required for bid forms to be signed by an individual legally empowered to bind the contractor to the owner in a legal contract. The bid documents should include all pertinent information from construction and design documents, so that bidding contractors can give a fair and accurate estimate.

Bid security

Sometimes a client and interior designer will determine that it is necessary to arrange bid security. In most cases, bid security is used to ensure that the selected bidder will enter into a contract with the owner. The form of security could be a certified check, bid bond, or cashier's check. If for some reason the successful bidder backs out, the bid security can be retained to compensate for the difference between the low bid and the next lowest bid. Usually, the amount of the bid security is either a fixed price or a percentage of the bid.

Copyright © Mometrix Media. You have been licensed one copy of this document for personal use only. Any other reproduction or redistribution is strictly prohibited. All rights reserved.

Bid contract substitutions

Some bid contracts will contain what are known as substitutions. Substitutions are conditions under which the owner will consider allowing alternate materials to be used. The substitutions portion of a bid contract typically indicates the owner's protocol for reviewing proposed substitutions. Substitution requests typically require the name of the material along with detailed information about it. At all times, the burden of proof rests with the bidders. When a substitution is approved, the owner will issue an addendum to all of the bidders. A contractor can propose substitutions during bidding so long as bidders request written approval at least 10 days before the bid opening. The request for written approval requires proof that the proposal fulfills the standards set by the contract documents.

Bidding process failure

It is important to remember that an interior designer and his or her client are not required to select one of the bids. In some cases, all the bids made on a project will be more than the budget allotted for the project by the owner. In this case, the owner can opt to rebid the contract. The owner may also decide to increase the budget for construction, or to select a contractor and attempt to reduce the price of the project. Occasionally, the building owner will have to simply abandon the project.

Bidding documents

Interior designers need to be well skilled in the art of composing bidding documents. Bidding documents are typically prepared by the designer, using either a standard form or a form provided by the owner. An owner who has arranged a number of different projects is likely to have a pre-established set of bidding documents. These documents are not considered a legal part of the contract document set. Bidding documents typically include an advertisement or invitation to bid, instructions to bidders, bid forms, bid security information, requirements for a performance bond, and any requirements for a labor and material payment bond.

An owner must play the most important role during the pre-bid period. At a pre-bid conference, the designer, owner, architect, consultants, and bidders will gather together so that the bidders can ask questions and the designer and owner can emphasize the important features of the project. The owner retains the right to reject any and all bids, specifically any incomplete bids or bids which are not accompanied by the required bid bond or other documentation. In situations where all of the bids exceed the project budget and the owner-designer agreement limits construction costs, the owner can do four things: rebid, authorize an increase in the construction cost, revise the scope of the project to reduce the cost, or abandon the project.

Copyright © Mometrix Media. You have been licensed one copy of this document for personal use only. Any other reproduction or redistribution is strictly prohibited. All rights reserved.

Bidding document alternatives

In some cases, an interior designer will be asked to include a set of alternates along with the bidding documents. Alternates are forms that ask each bidding contractor to supply a price for some type of variation from the base bid. In other words, the owner asks each contractor to adjust his or her bid based on some potential change in the project. This allows the owner to retain some flexibility over the cost of a project after bids have been submitted. Alternates are usually included when it seems likely that there will be some variation in the materials and methods available to the contractor after the contract has been awarded.

Bidder instructions

The instructions given to bidders usually contain the following information: procedures for submitting bids, source of bidding documents, procedure for opening bids, submittal information required with bid, representation statements of bidders, required bonds, and protocol for addenda. In bidding documents, unit prices are the set costs for certain portions of the work based on quantities like linear feet or square yards of installed material. In a bidding document, an addendum is a written or graphic document produced by the designer before the execution of a contract that modifies or specifically interprets the bidding documents by making additions, deletions, clarifications, or corrections. Addenda are issued during the bidding process before bids have been submitted. Sometimes an owner will request a certified check, bid bond, or cashier's check as insurance that the winning bidder will execute the contract.

Contract negotiation

Sometimes an interior designer and client may find that it is best to negotiate contracts. In a negotiated contract, the owner of the building picks a contractor and negotiates with him or her the terms of the contract. The four main advantages of negotiating a contract are that the owner can use a specific contractor, that a realistic project cost can be established from the beginning, that the contractor can help to reduce overall cost, and that the contractor can identify design problems. This method of establishing a contract works best when the owner and the contractor know one another and have worked together in the past.

Contract changes

The process of composing and making changes to interior design contract documents has a specific protocol. The documents are typically composed by the designer in consultation with the owner, although some owners may have pre-fabricated document forms. Four of the written changes that can be made after the execution of a contract are a change order, a written order for small changes in the project, amendments to the contract, and a written interpretation by the interior designer. All of these changes must be approved by both parties in order to be valid.

Copyright © Mometrix Media. You have been licensed one copy of this document for personal use only. Any other reproduction or redistribution is strictly prohibited. All rights reserved.

The written interpretation is a clarification of some design element that will affect the project timeline or budget.

Owner-vendor agreement

An incipient interior designer needs to be familiar with the basic provisions of the owner-vendor agreement. The major provisions of the agreement are the identification of contract documents, basic provisions, and progress payments. Contract documents typically consist of the following: the owner-contractor agreement, the general conditions of the contract, the supplementary conditions of the contract, drawings, specifications, addenda issued before execution, and modifications issued after execution. Bidding documents are not considered part of the set of contract documents. Progress payment protocol is always included in the owner-vendor agreement because it has the potential to become a contentious issue.

The three basic parts of an owner-vendor agreement are the identification of contract documents, the provisions of the contract, and the protocol for progress payments. In the agreement, it is declared that the contract documents will include the agreement, the contract conditions, the drawings, the schedules, and any subsequent addenda or modifications. The basic provisions of the contract include a description of the work, the date of commencement, the date of substantial completion, and the contract sum. The protocol for progress payments should include the number of days until payment after the application for payment has been made, as well as the conditions under which discounts, cancellations, or restocking fees can be assessed.

An interior designer may be required to supervise the addition to an owner-vendor agreement of specifications, addenda, and changes made after the execution of the contract. Specifications provide more detail to the methods and materials of the project. A manufacturer will often ask for clarification before signing a contract. Addenda modify the terms of the contract and are usually made after consultation and negotiation between client, designer, and vendor. Likewise, any changes made after the execution of the contract must be approved by all three parties. The forms on which all of these modifications and additions are made should be listed in the identification of contract documents at the beginning of the agreement.

Owner-contractor agreement

An interior designer needs to be familiar with the basic terms of an owner-contractor agreement. An owner-contractor agreement typically consists of three parts: an identification of contract documents, the basic provisions of the contract, and the protocol for progress payments. The first part identifies the following elements of the contract: agreement, contract conditions, drawings, schedules, specifications, and addenda. The basic provisions of the contract are the work to be done, the dates of commencement and substantial completion, and the total amount

Copyright © Mometrix Media. You have been licensed one copy of this document for personal use only. Any other reproduction or redistribution is strictly prohibited. All rights reserved.

to be paid to the contractor. It is typical for an owner to pay a contractor on a monthly basis, although this must be explicitly stated in the owner-contractor agreement.

An owner-vendor agreement always contains a summary of how liquidated damages and progress payments will be handled. Liquidated damages are any amounts of money that have to be paid by the contractor to the owner for every day the project is overdue. These represent the actual anticipated losses the owner will incur if the project is not completed on time. The calculation of liquidated damages is usually accompanied by a bonus provision so that the contractor will receive extra payment for early completion. When a penalty clause is included, a bonus provision must be included. Progress payments are periodic payments from the owner to the contractor, based on the completion of payment applications. The amount of the payment is based on the percentage of completed work and any materials purchased and stored. Vendors and contractors fill out an Application for Payment form to request payment from the owner.

Furniture, furnishings, and equipment

The owner is responsible for making adequate facilities available for delivery, staging, and storage of the above listed items. The owner must make sure all delivery and staging areas and delivery routes are free from obstacles or any other factors that may hinder the contractor. The owner must provide a contractor with a strict schedule for the use of unloading facilities and elevators. The owner should also inspect the work when it arrives to determine whether materials, furniture, and equipment are in good condition and in the right quantity.

The owner's inspection upon delivery should not be considered final, as the owner still retains the right to reject a shipment. The owner is also responsible for abiding by the agreed-upon critical dates in the progress schedule submitted by the contractor. The owner is responsible for providing security against loss or damage of furniture and equipment that is stored at the site between the time of delivery and the final acceptance by the owner. The owner is responsible for making the acceptance inspection of furniture and fixtures. Finally, and perhaps most importantly, only an owner can authorize the termination of a construction project.

During the installation of furniture, furnishings, and equipment, the contractor is responsible for selecting the routes to be used from the delivery points to the final destination. The contractor is also responsible for informing the owner about any special equipment or services that will be required for the proper delivery and installation of the work. The contractor and his employees should do all the cutting, fitting, or patching necessary to complete the work and should not change the work of any other people without getting the written consent of the owner. The contractor is required to provide labor, means, and methods of carrying out the work according to the prevailing labor conditions at the job site.

Copyright © Mometrix Media. You have been licensed one copy of this document for personal use only. Any other reproduction or redistribution is strictly prohibited. All rights reserved.

Furniture, furnishings, and equipment contract

Interior designers are often called upon to look over the contracts for furniture, furnishings, and equipment (FF&E). Therefore, they need to be aware of the common terms included therein. This document will be included in both the owner-vendor agreement and the owner-designer agreement. FF&E contracts are quite complicated, but almost always contain the following information: the definitions used by the purchaser and the vendor, the insurance required by each party, and the process of shipping and delivery. A contract for furniture, furnishings, and equipment must be composed in alignment with the Uniform Commercial Code in order to be considered valid.

UCC

Contracts related to furniture, furnishings, and equipment are subject to the provisions of the Uniform Commercial Code (UCC). The UCC applies to the sale and transfer of goods in the United States. It applies to transactions involving furniture and other movables. According to the UCC, furniture and accessories may be shipped by common carriers, contract carriers, or private carriers. Common carriers are those who offer their services to the general public. Contract carriers provide service only to certain companies with which they have elected to do business. Private carriers own and operate their own trucks to move their own merchandise.

FOB shipping

When a shipment is described as free on board (FOB), this means that the manufacturer will pay for loading the goods onto the delivery vehicle. When a shipment is described as free on board factory, title will be transferred at the factory, the buyer will pay for transportation costs, and the manufacturer will not be responsible for any loss or damage during shipping. When a shipment is described as FOB destination, this means that the manufacturer is responsible for shipping and for recovering any damage or loss during shipment. When a shipment is described as FOB factory freight prepaid, the furniture, furnishings, and equipment contractor owns the furniture but the manufacturer pays the shipping charges.

Contract for construction

An interior designer needs to be aware of the general conditions found in a contract for construction. The standard document for this purpose has been developed by the American Institute of Architects. Interior designers will typically use this version of the contract for construction, simply substituting the word "interior designer" for the word "architect." The general conditions of the contract generally cover the following topics: respective responsibilities of the designer, owner, and contractor; contract time; payment protocol; protection of persons and property; policy for changes in the work; and policies for the correction of faulty work.

Copyright © Mometrix Media. You have been licensed one copy of this document for personal use only. Any other reproduction or redistribution is strictly prohibited. All rights reserved.

An interior designer needs to be familiar with the common supplementary conditions in a construction contract. The Supplementary Conditions section of a contract agreement often contains those unique contract elements that can change the General Conditions of the Contract for Construction. Supplementary conditions will contain any information that is unique to the project. It may be placed in one of the following four areas on the contract:

- Bidding requirements: Conditions are placed here when they are related to bidding.
- Owner-contractor agreement: Conditions are placed here when they are related to contractual matters.
- Supplementary conditions: Conditions are placed here when they modify the general conditions.
- Division 1 of the specifications in the project menu.

There are a few common supplementary conditions that are found in many construction contracts. Common supplementary conditions include the following:

- additional information and services that will be provided by the owner
- an arrangement in which the owner will pay for utilities rather than the contractor
- fast-track scheduling
- criteria for liquidated damages and bonuses
- any additional specifications regarding payment protocol
- bonding and insurance specifications
- cost required for the architect to review substitution requests
- permission for the architect to provide instruments of service to the contractor in electronic form

Change order timing

Because unforeseen events are so common during an interior design, it is often necessary to modify the materials, methods, and schedule outlined in the original contract documents. An interior designer will prepare a change order to authorize changes in contract time and/or contract cost after the execution of the contract. A change order must be signed by the contractor, designer, and owner. Any time there is a modification of the contract cost or time, a change order is mandatory. Contract time is defined as the interval from the starting date established in the contract to the date of substantial completion. Contract time may be extended with a change order if delays beyond the contractor's control make it impossible to abide by the original duration.

Submittal protocol

There is a standard protocol for acquiring approval on submittals from suppliers and subcontractors. A submittal form will be sent to a general contractor. The general contractor will review it and forward it to the interior designer to be

Copyright © Mometrix Media. You have been licensed one copy of this document for personal use only. Any other reproduction or redistribution is strictly prohibited. All rights reserved.

approved. It may also be sent to any pertinent consultants for review. The submittal will then be sent back to the contractor who will in turn give it to the subcontractor or supplier who made the submittal. A submittal may be composed of shop drawings, samples, or product data. Shop drawings, which must be approved by the interior designer and the contractor, indicate the precise means by which a subcontractor or supplier will fulfill the stated obligations as per the contract.

Indemnification clauses

Interior designers try to minimize their exposure to third-party claims by including indemnification clauses in their contracts. Indemnification clauses seek to absolve the owner and interior designer of responsibility for any damages, claims, or losses caused by poor performance by individuals or groups with whom the interior designer does not have a contractual relationship. These clauses try to protect the owner and designer from claims made due to the negligence of the contractor or anyone working under the supervision of the contractor. However, in some cases an interior designer or owner can still be considered liable if it is determined that he or she did not give adequate instructions or failed to provide safe working conditions.

Mediation and arbitration

On occasion, an interior designer may need to assist the owner during a process of mediation or arbitration. These techniques are necessary when a claim cannot be resolved by the interior designer. In the process of mediation, a neutral third party helps develop a nonbinding agreement between the disputants. In the process of arbitration, a neutral third party renders a binding decision after hearing both arguments. In other words, the disputing parties are not required to accept the verdict of a mediator, but are required to abide by the verdict of an arbitrator.

Rescinding the contract

In California, a contract may be rescinded if all of the parties to the contract consent. However, a contract can also be rescinded by one party in a number of different circumstances. For instance, one party can rescind a contract if that party's original consent was obtained by mistake, fraud, duress, or any other undue influence. Also, a party can rescind a contract unilaterally if the consideration due that party for consent is not given. If the consideration becomes void or fails in a material respect, the receiving party may rescind the contract. If the contract is determined to be unlawful somehow, and if the unfairness is not equal among the parties, the disadvantaged party may rescind. Finally, if the execution of a contract will prejudice the public interest, a contract may be rescinded by one party.

Copyright © Mometrix Media. You have been licensed one copy of this document for personal use only. Any other reproduction or redistribution is strictly prohibited. All rights reserved.

Business Procedures

Acquiring capital

An interior designer needs to be familiar with the various ways that capital for a design project can be acquired. One way to acquire capital is through a loan. Secured loans require collateral in case of nonpayment, while unsecured loans do not require any collateral as a guarantee of payment. Designers can also pursue equity capital, which is any funding for a business that comes from investors. Venture capital, on the other hand, is funding specifically directed to a start-up business. Finally, an interior design firm might seek funds from an angel investor, an entrepreneur who invests in interior design businesses in part to help support another small business owner.

Credit

An interior designer needs to understand the various ways that a professional can use credit. Sometimes an interior design firm will establish a business plan and predict the potential for success. Using these financial projections to obtain credit is known as pursuing a pro forma credit policy. Trade credit, on the other hand, is the acquisition of materials from a supplier on the promise of later payment. Many fledgling interior design firms need to use trade credit and use their personal belongings as collateral. This is a risky form of credit and should only be pursued in cases where subsequent earnings are guaranteed.

Insurance coverage

There are a number of places where an interior designer can acquire insurance. One source is an independent insurance agent. This agent works with multiple insurance companies to provide the best possible coverage for individual clients. Another option is an exclusive agent. This type of agent works with only one insurance company and tends to be more knowledgeable about the plans offered. The exclusive agent does not offer the broad selections of an independent agent. The last choice is an insurance broker. Brokers work at the behest of the individual client and not in the service of any particular insurance company.

Copyright © Mometrix Media. You have been licensed one copy of this document for personal use only. Any other reproduction or redistribution is strictly prohibited. All rights reserved.

Charging for services

Interior designers may charge for their services based on a fixed fee or an hourly rate.

- Fixed fee: The client agrees to pay a specific sum of money to the designer for a specific set of services. Payment is usually made on a monthly basis. The designer establishes the sum of money based on costs, including salaries of employees, benefits, taxes, and office overhead. Reimbursable expenses are added in addition to the fees for basic services.

- Hourly rate: The client agrees to pay a set rate for each hour the designer spends on the project.

Interior designers often charge for services based on a percentage of the project cost. This method is best suited to projects in which the designer can accurately anticipate the amount of work that will be required, as well as the probable cost of the project. This is not a good idea when the project is on a small budget. On occasion, a client may be suspicious that the designer will be encouraged to increase the cost of the project in order to increase the professional fees or that the designer may lose the incentive to reduce construction and furnishings costs.

Interior designers sometimes base their service fees on a rate per area planned or designed or on the resale of wholesale furniture purchases.

Rates per area (square footage) planned or designed: Calculated by multiplying the square footage of the project by a fixed rate. Typically used in commercial construction. Protects the interests of the designer. The scope of services must be clearly defined.

Reselling wholesale furniture purchases at retail prices: In this scenario, the designer purchases furniture, fixtures, and other items at a trade discount and then sells them to the client at retail price. The difference in price amounts to the professional fees of the designer. This method is not recommended and is only used sparingly.

Calculating fees

Occasionally, an interior designer uses the multiple of direct personnel expense to calculate fees. In this method, normal personnel expenses are calculated by multiplying the direct hourly salary of employees by some factor representative of taxes, sick leave, health care, and other expenses. The resulting hourly amount has been increased by another multiplier (usually between 2.75 and 3) that includes provisions for overhead and profit. The multiplier must be agreed upon ahead of

Copyright © Mometrix Media. You have been licensed one copy of this document for personal use only. Any other reproduction or redistribution is strictly prohibited. All rights reserved.

time by the designer and the client. This method of calculating fees is only used on large-scale projects and by established designers.

The multiple of direct salary expense is similar to the method of multiple of direct personnel expense except that the multiplier is larger to account for employee benefits as well as overhead. Also, profit is based on direct hourly wage. The hourly method is preferred by designers because it ensures that every hour will be paid for and profitable. This method also protects the designer in cases where the client continually changes his or her mind or delays the completion of the job in some other way. Clients, on the other hand, may be uncomfortable with the open-ended nature of the hourly system and may seek to impose a maximum payment upon initiation of the contract.

Copyright © Mometrix Media. You have been licensed one copy of this document for personal use only. Any other reproduction or redistribution is strictly prohibited. All rights reserved.

Design Theory

Design elements

The six elements of design are form, color, scale, texture, pattern, and light. Form is the basic shape and configuration of an object or space. It is generated with lines, planes, volumes, and points. However, there are other factors that can influence the perception of form. For instance, the quantity and direction of light on an object influences one's perception of its size and shape. Similarly, differences in form can be emphasized or hidden through the use of color. Designers often seek to accentuate the differences in form between two objects by using wildly different colors.

Scale elements

Scale is the size of an object or elements of design in comparison to another object or element. Most commonly in interior design, the human body is the object to which other design elements are compared. Savvy designers use differences in scale to their advantage when making their plans. For instance, if a designer wants to make a cavernous room seem less forbidding, he or she might place some tall indoor plants in the corners of the room, so as to diminish the roomy feel of the space. Another way to make a large room seem less large is to enlarge the windows and doorways. This takes some of the viewer's attention off of the large dimensions of the room.

Color elements

In order to select an appropriate color scheme for a design project, an interior designer needs to know the basic elements of color. For instance, some colors are additive and some are subtractive. Colors that are created through the primary colors of light are red, green, and blue. In pigment, however, the true primary colors are yellow, magenta, and cyan. Hue is defined as the basic color, while value is defined as the degree of lightness or darkness related to black and white. Intensity, otherwise known as chroma, is the degree of color purity as compared to a neutral gray with the same value. Tint is the process of adding white to a particular hue, shade is the process of adding black to a particular hue, and tone is the process of adding gray or the complementary color to a given hue.

Color systems

The two major color systems are the Brewster and the Munsell. In the Brewster color system, also known as the Prang color system, the various colors are organized according to the three primary colors: red, blue, and yellow. When two primary colors are mixed together, secondary colors are formed. Specifically, yellow

Copyright © Mometrix Media. You have been licensed one copy of this document for personal use only. Any other reproduction or redistribution is strictly prohibited. All rights reserved.

and blue combine to make green. Yellow and red combine to make orange. Red and blue combine to make violet. These secondary colors combine with primary colors to form tertiary colors. The Munsell color system, on the other hand, defines color according to hue, value, and chroma. According to this system, there are five principal hues: yellow, green, blue, purple, and red. There are also five secondary hues. The ten total hues are broken down into four parts and given a number indicating the degree of saturation.

Color schemes

Interior designers need to be familiar with the following color schemes:
- Monochromatic: There is only one hue, with slight variations in intensity and value. This tends to result in a stark or intense effect.
- Analogous: Composed of hues which are close to one another on the color wheel.
- Complementary: Composed of hues that are on opposite sides of the color wheel.
- Triad: Incorporates three hues that are spaced evenly around the color wheel.
- Tetrad: Incorporates four hues that are spaced evenly around the color wheel.

Texture elements

Because interior design is primarily considered as a visual discipline, many designers overlook the importance of texture. Texture is the one design element that can be perceived with both touch and sight. Texture is the surface quality of a material. Designers differentiate between actual and visual texture. Actual texture is the physical quality that is sensed through touch. Visual texture, on the other hand, is what we imagine the texture of the surface to be when we look at it. A smooth or glossy texture reflects light, creates glare, and demonstrates the imperfections in the surface. A rough or matte texture diffuses and absorbs light.

Light components

Designers must be aware of the basic principles of light if they want to effectively illuminate a space. To begin with, the designer needs to know the amount of light that is required based on the activities that will be accomplished within the space. For instance, an elegant restaurant will probably require less lighting than an office environment. The designer also needs to be aware of the quality of light that is present in a space. The three primary colors of light are red, green, and blue. Depending on the type of glazing that is used, an interior designer can accentuate each of these colors.

Copyright © Mometrix Media. You have been licensed one copy of this document for personal use only. Any other reproduction or redistribution is strictly prohibited. All rights reserved.

Design principles

The six principles of design are: emphasis and focus, harmony and unity, contrast and variety, rhythm, proportion, and balance. Balance is the arrangement of elements in a composition designed to achieve a sense of visual equilibrium. The relative weight of an object depends on the size and placement. There are three types of balance:
- Symmetrical balance: Identical elements are ranged equally around a common axis. This type of balance creates a stable formality.
- Asymmetrical balance: Achieved by arranging unlike elements in such a way that the overall composition is balanced. This balance occurs despite the fact that the elements are not grouped around a common axis.
- Radial balance: The regular arrangement of elements around some central point.

Harmony and unity

Interior designers are constantly striving to achieve harmony in their designs. Harmony is the agreement of the parts in a composition with one another. In other words, elements do not clash with one another, but are similar to one another. An interior design is said to have harmony when all the elements work together to develop a unified theme. For instance, a designer will often replicate the same shape or pattern throughout design in order to create harmony. A similar concept, unity, is achieved by maintaining some similarity between all the design elements in a space. Objects seem to fit or to belong together.

Rhythm

When interior designers refer to the principle of rhythm in their compositions, they do not mean the percussive element of music. Rhythm is the repetition of elements in a composition in a regular pattern. Gradation is a subcategory of rhythm. It is used to identify design elements in which the size, color, or value has been subtly altered. Interior designers also know that they can draw attention to a certain element in the design by disrupting a rhythm. For instance, if the designer wants to draw the eye towards a certain chair, like the one in which the leader of the gathering will be sitting, he might place a number of similarly-sized chairs to either side, with a much larger or different-colored chair in the middle.

Proportion

Interior designers must remain conscious of the design principle of proportion as they outline a project. Proportion is the relationship between one part of an object or composition to another part or to the whole composition. It is important for a designer to understand the effects that are generated by the proportions of different elements in a composition. For instance, a piece of decorative artwork that seems

Copyright © Mometrix Media. You have been licensed one copy of this document for personal use only. Any other reproduction or redistribution is strictly prohibited. All rights reserved.

large when viewed in the designer's office may be dwarfed into obscurity by the dimensions of its final location. Proportion is the relative sizes of two different objects or elements, whereas scale is the relative size of an object or element with some other object of known size. When designers measure the size of something as it compares to the human body, they are dealing in scale. Proportion does not require comparison with an object of known size.

Interior designers need to understand some of the basic topics related to proportional design. One of the most well-known proportions is the golden ratio. That is, A is to B as B is to (A + B). This ratio can be expressed as 1.618 or 1 plus the square root of 5, with the resulting sum divided by 2. When applied to rectangles, this ratio is called the Golden Section. Another famous proportion is the Fibonacci sequence or the series of numbers beginning with zero and one, in which each subsequent number is the sum of the previous two numbers in the sequence. So, for instance, the Fibonacci sequence might proceed as 0, 1, 1, 2, 3, 5, 8. Finally, the modular proportioning system was developed by Le Corbusier. It uses the human body as its primary reference point. This system encourages designers to create spaces uniquely suited to the dimensions of the human body.

Patterns

In order to create designs that achieve the aesthetic ends of symmetry and harmony, an interior designer needs to use patterns in a sophisticated and conscious manner. A pattern is the repetition of some decorative element on a particular surface. Patterns can be created with furniture as well as with decorative elements. For instance, in a large space an interior designer could establish a pattern of groups of chairs, say, three chairs arranged around a small table. In like fashion, a designer could utilize the pattern embossed on wallpaper or paint to achieve a similar design end.

Emphasis and focus

To be successful, interior designers need to understand how to emphasize or draw focus to a particular element or space within the design project. There are a number of ways to accomplish this. Interior designers often achieve emphasis and focus by displaying a certain element in a prominent position or by lighting it in a particular way. An object can also be emphasized by being placed in the middle of the room or being set apart from the other objects around it. There are a number of reasons to emphasize certain elements of a design scheme: to demonstrate hierarchy or status, to draw the eye away from certain other design elements, or to showcase a particularly beautiful design component.

Contrast and variety

To enhance the value of the elements within a design composition, an interior designer will rely on the principles of contrast and variety. In interior design,

Copyright © Mometrix Media. You have been licensed one copy of this document for personal use only. Any other reproduction or redistribution is strictly prohibited. All rights reserved.

contrast is the art of placing unlike elements next to one another in order to emphasize a certain part of composition. Contrast is essentially the perception of differences between objects in the environment. Variety, on the other hand, is the intentional differentiation among the elements in a design. Except in rare cases, an interior designer will want to vary the elements of a design. Otherwise, the overall effect of the predominant element can be overwhelming or boring.

Speech privacy

The following are five common strategies for increasing speech privacy in a large area:
- Adding sound absorbent ceiling materials, such as perforated foam
- Incorporating space dividers composed of sound-absorbent materials, such as foam or fabric
- Placing loud activities far away from one another, so as to minimize sound interference
- Minimizing reflected sound by a careful arrangement of hard surfaces, taking care to not create echo chambers in which sounds can reverberate
- Utilizing a background masking system, which provides white noise and renders distant sound indistinct

Social and cultural

An interior designer will need to consider a number of social and cultural factors when planning a space. For instance, in some cultures it is considered inappropriate for males and females to mix together freely. An interior designer will then have to ensure that there are separate means of egress and facilities for males and females. Another example of cultural effects on interior design is regionalism, which is any element of design that is influenced by the style of a specific geographical area. For instance, the American Southwest has a unique design scheme influenced by the Spanish and Native American populations of that region.

Design concepts

A design concept is any idea related to the physical changes that will be made as a result of programming. A design concept is a statement of the specific physical plans for how a programmatic concept will be realized. In other words, a design concept is a more specific, realistic view of the possibilities for the project. It must take into account the existing conditions, that is, the size of the existing space, the views, plumbing, the structural considerations, and any special features. Some of the programming concepts may ultimately be determined to be impossible once design concepts have been examined and outlined.

Copyright © Mometrix Media. You have been licensed one copy of this document for personal use only. Any other reproduction or redistribution is strictly prohibited. All rights reserved.

Plan arrangements

When an interior designer is planning a large space, he or she needs to consider the degree to which people need to be separated or brought together. There are a number of classic plan arrangements that address this problem. They include the following:
- Open: Consists entirely of furniture and accessories without any partitions and does not allow for differentiation of lighting or privacy.
- Linear: A series of spaces or rooms placed in a single line. A very adaptable plan.
- Axial: Consists of two or more major linear segments with spaces and rooms placed throughout. An axial arrangement usually includes a featured termination at one or more ends of the axis.
- Centralized: Secondary elements are placed around a central axis or point. The appropriate conceptual plan arrangements for creating focused attention in a non-directional way. Especially useful in a formal space, such as a hotel lobby.
- Grid: Composed of two sets of space elements which may be perpendicular, at angles, and/or irregularly spaced. Can be very monotonous and confusing. Appropriate for very large spaces.
- Clustered: A number of spaces with similar size, shape, and function are linked through a central space or corridor. Quite close to one another.

Space relationships

One of the fundamental design problems that must be solved is the extent to which individuals housed within a common space should have their own personal areas. There are four basic space relationships that an interior designer can select:
- Adjacent spaces: The most common kind of space relationship. Every space has its own room and spaces are separated by some piece of construction, such as a wall.
- Overlapping spaces: Could be used to link two different spaces, both in appearance and function.
- Spaces sharing a common area: Each space has its own particular purpose and is linked to some common space.
- Space within another space: A particular space or room is carved out of a larger space.

Space allocation

Interior designers who agree to work on commercial buildings must observe certain restrictions regarding the allocation of space. The government mandates a number of specifications so that public buildings will be accessible to handicapped individuals. For instance, in a commercial building a corridor needs to be at least 44 inches wide, though it probably should be at least 60 inches wide. Besides these

Copyright © Mometrix Media. You have been licensed one copy of this document for personal use only. Any other reproduction or redistribution is strictly prohibited. All rights reserved.

concerns, an interior designer also needs to be aware of the location and size of the building facilities, so that he or she can leave enough space for maintenance workers.

Basic components

Three of the most basic elements of interior design are walls, ceilings, and floors:
- Walls: Perhaps the most important component of interior design, as they define spaces and are continually present to the eye. Walls are endlessly variable.
- Ceilings: Besides defining the upper boundaries of a space and making a space "interior," ceilings contain important mechanical and electrical components, like HVAC equipment, lighting and sprinkler systems.
- Floors: Exert a significant influence on the acoustic, aesthetic, and pragmatic features of a space. Flooring can also be used to help direct circulation throughout a give space.
- Steps: Allow for vertical transitions between horizontal spaces. Used effectively, steps can create drama or hierarchy in a design setting.
- Doors: Separate and connect different spaces. Depending on how they are used, doors can invite or forbid circulation between adjacent spaces. They can also indicate status or hierarchy.
- Windows: Like doors, windows can simultaneously connect and separate two spaces. Although windows are primarily used between interior and exterior spaces, they can also be used between interior spaces to create a feeling of connection and openness in a room.

Circulation patterns

Circulation patterns are guides to organizing a room, open space, or entire project. In order for a space to be organized efficiently and for people to be effectively oriented in the environment, the circulation pattern must be sensible and clear. There are three common circulation patterns:
- Dumbbell layout: The simplest and most adaptable circulation pattern. Spaces are arranged along a straight path connecting two major elements at each end.
- Doughnut layout: A double-loaded corridor functions as a continuous exit. Large spaces may thrive with this type of circulation pattern.
- Radial layout: Oriented around a single major space with paths extending from this area. Typical of situations where all activity centers around a single focal point.

When developing circulation patterns, a designer will typically develop a furnishings layout. This determines the types and numbers of individual pieces of furniture that will be required for a given space. It also takes into account the amount of space between the pieces of furniture, as well as their positioning in

Copyright © Mometrix Media. You have been licensed one copy of this document for personal use only. Any other reproduction or redistribution is strictly prohibited. All rights reserved.

relation to one another. For instance, the designer may want to place a group of chairs together so that people can gather and converse easily. On the other hand, the designer may want to arrange seating such that people will tend to sit quietly without talking to one another. At this point the designer is considering the general access to the furniture grouping, as well as its relationship to the elements that already are planned for the space.

Copyright © Mometrix Media. You have been licensed one copy of this document for personal use only. Any other reproduction or redistribution is strictly prohibited. All rights reserved.

Human Factors

Ergonomics

In order to make a space as human-friendly as possible, a designer needs to be familiar with the science of ergonomics. Ergonomics is the study of the interrelationships between the human body and the physical environment. Ergonomics incorporates some of the insights of anthropometrics, but spends more time focusing on the interactions of human beings with the physical world. The ability to adjust one's surroundings to one's own personal dimensions is a major focus of ergonomics. An ergonomic desk, for instance, allows the user to adjust the placement of the keyboard tray so that he or she can type in a comfortable position. The use of ergonomic equipment has been linked consistently with lower rates of repetitive stress injuries among office employees.

Anthropometrics

In order to arrange spaces in such a way that they are conducive to productive human activity, a designer needs to be familiar with the science of anthropometrics. Anthropometrics is the study of the size and mobility of the human body. Although human bodies come in all shapes and sizes, there are common proportions which remain consistent for all people. Designers use this information to determine the minimum and optimum dimensions required for an individual to perform certain activities. The field of anthropometrics is divided into both static and dynamic categories. Static anthropometrics considers the dimensions of the human body while at rest. Dynamic anthropometrics considers the measurements of the human body while it is in motion.

Comfort

Designers must constantly be attuned to the effects of their programming decisions on comfort. A human being's comfort level is based on the following factors: temperature, humidity, air movement, temperature radiation from surrounding surfaces, air quality, sound, vibration, and light. For the most part, people want to be warm and dry. The human body can lose heat through convection, evaporation, or radiation.

Convection is the transfer of heat through the movement of a gas or liquid. In general, greater air movement means more evaporation and more heat loss through convection. Evaporation is the conversion of moisture into a vapor as a result of perspiration or respiration. Radiation is the transfer of heat through electromagnetic waves, from the warmer surface to the colder surface. If the human body is warmer than its surroundings, it will naturally lose heat to the surroundings.

Copyright © Mometrix Media. You have been licensed one copy of this document for personal use only. Any other reproduction or redistribution is strictly prohibited. All rights reserved.

A primary concern of the interior designer is maintaining comfortable conditions in which to live and work. Air temperature is the primary determinant of comfort. For most people, a comfortable temperature range is between 69 and 80°F. Interior designers typically use what is known as effective temperature, which takes into account air temperature, humidity, and air movement. The interior designer must also consider relative humidity and wind speed. Relative humidity is the percentage of moisture in the air related to the maximum amount of moisture that the air could potentially hold at that temperature without condensing. For a human being, a comfortable range of relative humidity is between 30 and 65%. For human beings, wind speeds of between 50 and 200 feet per minute are acceptable for remaining cool without becoming uncomfortable.

In order to maintain comfortable temperature levels within an enclosed space, an interior designer needs to be familiar with the mean radiant temperature and the ventilation in the space. Mean radiant temperature is the measure of temperature change due to radiation in an individual. Designers use mean radiant temperature to determine the level of comfort in a room by finding out whether an individual is radiating or absorbing heat from the surrounding surfaces. Mean radiant temperature is calculated as a weighted average of sunlight and the surface temperatures of the various objects in the room. Ventilation is necessary to provide oxygen and remove carbon dioxide. A proper ventilation system also carries away odors and contaminants. The amount of ventilation needed in a particular room depends on what goes on there, the size of the room, and whether people are allowed to smoke there. It is possible for a room to be excessively ventilated, as when the ventilation results in a great deal of air flow.

Behavior settings and territoriality

A behavior setting is a specific place with recognizable boundaries and objects, in which a regular course of behavior takes place at a given time. An example of a behavior setting might be an office cubicle, which has strictly defined limits and in which a given individual regularly performs the same sort of tasks. Human beings are likely to develop a sense of territoriality in any space they inhabit frequently. Territoriality is the human attempt to impose self-identity on a space and develop a sense of ownership over it. Humans have an innate need to impose their identity on their environment and establish that they have a freedom of choice. Territoriality is expressed when an office worker hangs up pictures of her family or when a janitor arranges the equipment in his utility closet in a distinct way.

Proxemics

Proxemics is the study of the distances and relative positions maintained between people who are interacting with one another. People naturally, and for the most part unconsciously, assume different relative positions and distances from one another depending on their relationship. For designers, proxemics is used to determine how much space needs to be allowed between the people who will be operating in the

Copyright © Mometrix Media. You have been licensed one copy of this document for personal use only. Any other reproduction or redistribution is strictly prohibited. All rights reserved.

proposed space. The appropriate proxemics change depending on culture and level of familiarity. The 4 distances outlined in proxemics are, from closest to most distant are the following:

- Intimate: from zero to 18 inches
- Personal: from 18 inches to 4 feet
- Social: from 4 feet to 12 feet
- Public: greater than 12 feet

Maslow's hierarchy of needs

Interior designers often use Maslow's hierarchy of needs during the programming process. The American psychologist Abraham Maslow is credited with developing a system ranking the various human needs by importance. In order for a human being to satisfy his or her most elevated needs, which include self-actualization and beauty, his or her most basic needs must be satisfied. These basic needs include food, shelter, and water. The next most important needs are for safety, both physical and mental. The third level lists love and self-esteem.

Personalization

In interior design, personalization is the adjustment of the surrounding environment to an individual's preferences. Personalization is a manner of indicating a sense of territoriality over a particular space. In an office environment, for instance, people will bring personal effects as a means of making an otherwise impersonal space seem more relevant to their own lives. However, personalization also can be as simple as adjusting the furniture arrangements in the room to enhance one's own comfort. For instance, an individual who slides a chair over so that he can rest his feet on it is engaging in an act of personalization. During the programming process, interior designers will want to find out how much personalization the client wants to allow or make possible in the planned space.

Group interaction

Interior designers need to take into account the desired level of group interaction. If individuals are meant to interact closely with one another, chairs will be placed in close groups. Also, when individuals are meant to interact with one another, chairs will be positioned so that they face one another. If individuals are not supposed to interact with one another, chairs will be placed farther apart and will be positioned so that seated individuals do not directly face one another. In general, round tables are best for seating small groups in which there is no formal hierarchy. When the group is to be led by a particular individual, it is common practice to use a rectangular table, so that the leader can sit at the head.

Copyright © Mometrix Media. You have been licensed one copy of this document for personal use only. Any other reproduction or redistribution is strictly prohibited. All rights reserved.

Status

In ways both subtle and overt, interior design can indicate the relative power of the individuals who work and live in a space. For instance, in an office environment, the relative status of individual employees is often denoted by the size and position of an office. Obviously, the employees with larger offices are presumed to have a higher level of status within the organization. Corner offices are considered to have a higher status, mainly because they have two walls of windows. It should be noted that in some organizations there will be an emphasis on lessening differences in status. For instance, it is possible that the chief executive of an organization will want to boost morale among employees by working right alongside them without any obvious rewards for his or position. The interior designers should consult with the client as to whether there are any status-related requirements for the given project.

Copyright © Mometrix Media. You have been licensed one copy of this document for personal use only. Any other reproduction or redistribution is strictly prohibited. All rights reserved.

Design Phase

Design process

During the design process, an interior designer has to balance a number of competing interests. He/she needs to maintain the program adjacencies, maintain the division between public and private space and make sure that enclosed spaces are enclosed and open spaces are open. The development of a sound circulation pattern is essential to reconciling these various issues. Most interior designers believe that a linear layout is the most efficient and flexible type of circulation pattern. An interior designer may also devote much energy in the design process to questions of sustainability, particularly when encouraged to do so by the client. For instance, in commercial buildings, it is typical for 30% to 40% of the total energy use to be devoted to electric lighting and the associated cooling needs. An interior designer focused on sustainability will want to reduce this percentage as much as possible.

Design details

After an interior designer has selected the appropriate design details for a project, he or she needs to work in consultation with the clients to develop and design a plan that stays within budget while meeting the aesthetic needs and desires of the client. This process centers around the process of detailing--determining exactly how the various proposed elements in a design scheme will look together. In order to succeed in this process, a designer needs to consider whether each element in the design scheme is functional, structurally sound and aesthetically appropriate. Once these criteria have been met, the designer will need to determine whether each design element fits within the project budget.

Programming process

The programming process begins by defining the problem. The designer then develops a specific definition of the goals and objectives of the client. This preliminary period may involve analysis of the existing structure, aesthetic and space considerations for the project, adjacency requirements, code restrictions, scheduling limitations, and budget demands. During the programming process, all the information required to perform a project is collected and subjected to a rigorous analysis. An interior designer will need to cooperate with the owner and possibly with consultants during this period. Many interior designers examine records of past projects to generate ideas and discover limitations.

During the programming process, a designer will be concerned mainly with form, function, economy, and time. Form is the consideration of the existing conditions, both physical and psychological, in the building, as well as the potential quality of

Copyright © Mometrix Media. You have been licensed one copy of this document for personal use only. Any other reproduction or redistribution is strictly prohibited. All rights reserved.

construction. Function is the consideration of the people and activities to be housed within the space. Economy is the consideration of available money. A designer will need to understand what the owner can afford and what payment schedule will be possible. Time, finally, is the consideration of the duration available for design work.

An interior designer begins a project by executing the basic programming protocol. The five steps in the programming process are as follows: establish goals, collect facts, uncover concepts, determine needs, and state the problem. The facts collected during programming describe existing conditions and the following requirements for the proposed space: number of people, space adjacencies, user characteristics, equipment to be housed, expected growth rate, budget, and building codes. During the programming process, the designer is trying to develop abstract ideas that provide functional solutions to the problems of the client without necessarily defining the physical means that will be required to solve these problems.

During the phase of programming in which the designer is determining the needs of the client, the designer should take care to balance the desires of the client with the available budget. If the budget is not already established, the designer should develop it with the client on the basis of the defined goals or needs. It may be necessary to prioritize the goals of the client. A program format is a statement of goals and objectives--for instance, the number of people who will be in a space, the activities that will be performed in a space, etc. A program format may include specific tallies of spaces and their requisite square footage. Note that the program format does not indicate whether it will be possible to meet the desires of the client. Indeed, the next phase of the programming process requires the designer to list all of the potential obstacles to satisfactory completion of the project. In order for this phase to be effective, the client must be totally honest with the designer.

In order to effectively program, a designer needs to have the following information: client objectives, user requirements, activity requirements, furnishings and equipment adjacencies, space requirements, allotted time, and budget. There are a few ways to acquire this information. During the programming process, designers will engage in a bit of behavior observation in order to determine the appropriate characteristics of the proposed space. However, behavior observation is not a foolproof method of gathering information. For one thing, it is unable to attribute causes for the behavior that is observed. Finally, behavior observation is difficult to extrapolate; the behavior exhibited during a particular period of time may not be representative.

Obtaining information

During the programming process, designers will use the following four primary methods of obtaining information:
- Client interviews: An opportunity for the designer to deliver structured and specific questions, to clarify ambiguous areas, and to explore the needs and ideas of the client.

Copyright © Mometrix Media. You have been licensed one copy of this document for personal use only. Any other reproduction or redistribution is strictly prohibited. All rights reserved.

- Questionnaires: A written form consisting of a list of standard questions.
- Observation: A reliable method of gathering information, though observations taken during a very brief period should not be extrapolated too broadly. Best used in combination with interviews and questionnaires.
- Field surveys: Performed to determine the size and arrangement of the buildings, the existence of built-in structures, the location of nonbearing walls, the locations and sizes of doors, windows, and outlets, as well as the current plumbing and lighting fixtures. Field surveys can also be performed to determine ceiling conditions, potential noise problems, and any hazardous materials present in the building or space.

Design requirements

During the programming process, an interior designer will often have to research the design requirements for the structures and furnishings proposed for development in a space. Product information can be obtained from a number of different sources, but designers typically look for it in product catalogs, manufacturers' websites, trade association publications, documents produced by the representatives of the manufacturer, and in the *Sweets Catalog*. During the early phases of programming, a designer is likely to spend a great deal of time perusing catalogs and browsing showrooms. Once he or she has a more refined idea of what will be required for the project, manufacturers' representatives and consultants will be able to provide a more detailed description of products.

Space considerations

One of the most important tasks an interior designer has to perform during the programming process is the prediction of how much space will be required. When making this assessment, the two most important pieces of data are the required area and the adjacencies in the structure. There are a few different ways to calculate the required area in a structure. One is to multiply the area for one person by the total number of people in the area. This assumes that every person will need roughly the same amount of space. When this method is inappropriate, the amount of space can be determined by the amount of equipment that will fill the space or by the activity that will be performed in the space. A tennis court, for instance, requires a great deal more space for two people than does a set of office cubicles.

Interior designers use the following terms to describe the space considerations in a proposed project:
- Total required area: The full amount of space necessary to meet the demands of the client.
- Net area (or net assignable area): The amount of space required for a particular function. Does not include primary circulation space or support space (e.g., closets).

Copyright © Mometrix Media. You have been licensed one copy of this document for personal use only. Any other reproduction or redistribution is strictly prohibited. All rights reserved.

- Unassigned area: All of the space that does not contribute to the calculation of net assignable area. Unassigned areas include closets, exterior walls, and the building core.
- Primary circulation space: All of the public circulation spaces in a leased building, including the lobbies, corridors, and exits.
- Secondary circulation space: All of the corridors connecting net assignable area with primary circulation areas.
- Usable area: The area required for the intended purpose of the space. Also includes circulation spaces, partitions, and columns.
- Rentable area: All the area within the perimeter walls which can be rented to a tenant. May also include private hallways, columns, walls, a share of restrooms, a share of elevator lobbies, and a share of public corridors. When an entire floor is rented, the rentable area includes all the space taken by public corridors, restrooms, and lobbies on the floor.
- Gross area: The sum total of new area and ancillary areas.
- Efficiency factor: The ratio between one area and another. Used to determine the amount of space required for a given activity.
- Rentable-usable ratio: Rentable area divided by usable area. Used to calculate the total amount of space required given a certain amount of usable area.
- Interior layout efficiency ratio: Ratio of net area to usable area in a leased space.
- Overall building efficiency: Ratio of net assignable area to gross building area.
- Space planning efficiency ratio: Equal to the ratio of the net to gross ratio. Usually between 60% and 80%.
- Exit number: In order to calculate the number of exits required for a space, a designer will need to know the floor area and the size of the occupancy group.

Programming report

A programming report will need to include the following information: title page, introduction, executive summary, explanation of report goals and objectives, summary of space needs, space adjacency requirements, code requirements, analysis of existing space, budget and schedule requirements, programming concepts, and appendices. The summary of space needs will include existing staff and staff projections, workflow analysis, equipment needs, and a tabulation of space needs with circulation. The space adjacency section will include adjacency matrices, bubble diagrams, and, for multiple-story projects, stacking diagrams. The analysis of existing space will include architectural space configurations and structural, mechanical, electrical, and safety requirements. The appendices often include detailed space needs tabulation, inventory of existing furniture, and information about any other surveys.

Copyright © Mometrix Media. You have been licensed one copy of this document for personal use only. Any other reproduction or redistribution is strictly prohibited. All rights reserved.

Contract Documents

Construction drawings

Construction drawings are used by contractors and subcontractors to help on a construction project. Construction drawings indicate the positions, dimensions, and interrelations of construction elements. The basic set of construction drawings contains, in order, the following: title and index sheet, floor plans, reflected ceiling plans, elevations, details, mechanical drawings, electrical drawings, and fire protection drawings. Note that this is simply a list of the construction drawings that are relevant to the work of an interior designer. There may be additional forms surrounding these if the project in question also involves external construction.

Interior designers need to be familiar with the characteristics and contents of the following construction drawings:
- Title and index sheet: Includes the index, a list of standard abbreviations, project data, the square footage, the occupancy category, and the building type, among other things.
- Floor plans: Includes demo plans, construction plans, finish plans, telephone and power plan, and furniture plans. A floor plan provides views of the building as if it were cut horizontally four feet above the floor. It shows building configuration, including walls, dimensions, existing construction, references to elevations and details, room names and numbers, floor material indications, millwork, plumbing fixtures, built-in fixtures and stairs. A floor plan also indicates the general configuration of the building being worked on, including any doors, partitions, or other fixed elements. A floor plan should include dimensions and elevation details.
- Demolition plans: Indicates the existing construction that will remain and the existing construction that will be removed.
- Site plans: Provides a view of the building as seen from directly overhead. Includes roof, surrounding grounds, and any other features within the property line. Often includes the streets and properties immediately adjacent to the site.
- Reflected ceiling plans: Provides a view of the ceiling as if it were reflected by a mirror placed on the floor. Details any design components that have to do with the ceiling, including those elements which simply touch the ceiling.
- Elevations: Indicates the vertical dimensions of an area, including the finishes and configurations of the walls.
- Details: Small-scale, specific renderings of particular elements of construction. Examples of common subjects of details include millwork, flooring, glazing, ceilings, doors, and stairs. The more competitive the bidding process is, the more detailed the drawings should be.
- Mechanical drawings: Any drawings that would be necessary for a mechanical engineering consultant to complete the job. For instance, any

- 72 -

Copyright © Mometrix Media. You have been licensed one copy of this document for personal use only. Any other reproduction or redistribution is strictly prohibited. All rights reserved.

requisite information about the heating, ventilation, or air-conditioning systems.
- Electrical drawings: Any drawings that would be necessary for an electrical engineering consultant to complete the job. May include light fixture and switch locations, circuitry, and any specialty wiring.
- Fire protection drawings: In buildings that require a sprinkler system, these drawings must be composed by a mechanical engineer.

Drafting of construction drawings

There are certain standards in the drafting of construction drawings with which interior designers need to be familiar, even if they will not be developing the drawings themselves. There is no standard sheet size; firms use a particular size based on their filing system and the types of jobs they usually do. The three standard sizes are based on architectural, American National Standards Institute, and International Standards Organization systems. Title blocks typically contain the basic information about the project, as well as the sheet number, sheet name, and revision dates. There is a narrow binding edge on the left side of the sheet. The main body of the sheet is the drawing area. Along the right margin, the following sections are arranged from top to bottom: project information, designer information, approval stamps, revisions, sheet title, and sheet number. Finally, layering is the technique of separating information by level in a CAD system.

Construction drawings coordination

An interior designer needs to be able to coordinate basic construction drawings with the specific drawings composed by consultants. Plumbing, electrical, fire protection and security consultants all need to be in communication so that their construction plans do not interfere with one another. Ultimately, however, the interior designer is responsible for coordinating these construction drawings. In order to make sure that their drawings do not interfere with one another, consultants need to have access to structural drawings, mechanical and plumbing drawings, and electrical drawings. The basis for effective coordination is the establishment of a good communication system and the constant monitoring of communication among the various parties.

Reference system

The reference marks used in construction drawings are basically consistent and need to be known to an interior designer so that these documents can be read accurately. The three most important reference marks to know are the elevation, section, and detail. On an elevation reference mark, the top number is the detail number, while the bottom number refers to the particular sheet on which the given elevation is drawn. A section reference mark indicates where a perpendicular view of some piece of the construction has been given. A detail reference mark indicates

- 73 -

Copyright © Mometrix Media. You have been licensed one copy of this document for personal use only. Any other reproduction or redistribution is strictly prohibited. All rights reserved.

the part of the larger drawing that has been isolated and drawn in greater detail. As with the other reference marks, the top number identifies the detail, and the bottom number indicates the page on which the detail is drawn.

Permitting and contracting process

An interior designer needs to be familiar with the appropriate requirements for forms during the permitting and contracting process. Building departments usually require the following information: location, nature, and extent of the proposed work; location plan; comprehensive key glass descriptions; indication of fire rated partitions, doors and other openings; locations of exit signs and fire extinguishers; fire protection shop drawings; structural calculations; mechanical and electrical drawings; specifications regarding products, materials, finishes; and test standards. Whatever authority has jurisdiction over a construction site will issue a Certificate of Occupancy (occasionally known as a Certificate of Use and Occupancy) which gives permission to the client to occupy the allotted space after final inspection. In addition, it may be necessary to provide the codes being used; the occupant load calculations; sprinkler system plans; the names and addresses of all the design professionals working on the job; the street address of the project; framing inspection forms; gypsum wallboard inspection forms; plumbing, mechanical, and electrical inspection forms; and a final inspection form.

Evaluating materials and products

An interior designer needs to consider structural safety, fire retardants, and safety of human contact when selecting construction materials and detailing. These considerations should be made in light of the activities that will be taking place in the project space. For instance, the wood finish in a nightclub had better be more flame-retardant than that in an office environment. Also, the interior designer needs to work in consultation with the owner to ensure that all the materials and processes to be used stay within the agreed-upon budget and meet the designated criteria for function and durability.

Evaluating building codes

Before construction can begin on a project, the interior designer needs to make sure that the proposed plan does not violate any relevant building codes or regulations. Building codes mandate certain specifications for corridors, stairways, ramps, interior glazing, exit signs, and other safety-related features. Also, during the detailing process an interior designer needs to keep in mind the following causes of building movements: temperature change, water absorption, dead load deflection, live load deflection, and lateral loading caused by wind or earthquakes. There are specific regulations designed to prevent these loads from doing damage to the structure of a building.

Copyright © Mometrix Media. You have been licensed one copy of this document for personal use only. Any other reproduction or redistribution is strictly prohibited. All rights reserved.

SDS

Manufacturers are required to produce a safety data sheet (SDS, formerly MSDS), in which the physical composition, proper storage and handling, and other safety-related characteristics of a product are described. An SDS basically describes the safety hazards associated with a given material or process. For instance, the SDS accompanying fiberglass insulation will contain a warning about the dangers of inhaling this substance. These forms are required by OSHA and must contain information about any features that have the potential for short-term and long-term harm.

Scheduling

One of an interior designer's most important and complex tasks is arranging the various phases of the project in such a way as to minimize wasted time and money. Scheduling needs to take into account two phases: design time and construction and installation time. The designer is responsible for developing a schedule for the design of the job, and the production of contract documents. The contractor, meanwhile, is responsible for scheduling construction. The amount of time required will depend on the following factors: the size and complexity of the project, the number of people working on the project, the type of decision-making and approval processes agreed upon by the client and designer, and any fixed dates, such as move-in dates or lease expiration. In general, the more independence the designer is given by the client, the faster the project can be completed. In the development of a total project schedule, the contractor is responsible for estimating the entire construction time. However, this can only be done in close consultation with other contractors and the designer.

An interior designer typically relies on Gantt charts and critical path method schedules during the scheduling process. A Gantt chart resembles a bar graph. It is the most common form of scheduling, in which different activities are plotted on a vertical axis, timeline, or horizontal axis. Each activity is assigned a start and finish date. This type of chart is appropriate for small and medium-sized projects, but it cannot show all sequences or the dependencies of one activity on another. A critical path method (CPM) schedule shows the tasks required to complete the project, as well as the sequence in which they must occur, their duration, and their earliest or latest possible start and finish times. A CPM schedule indicates the sequence of tasks that are critical or that must be started and finished precisely on time if the total schedule is to be fulfilled.

Project manual

There is a standard organizational structure for project manuals. A project manual contains the following information: bidding requirements, supplemental bid forms, contract forms, general and supplementary conditions, and technical specifications. The bidding requirements section of the manual will include an invitation to bid,

Copyright © Mometrix Media. You have been licensed one copy of this document for personal use only. Any other reproduction or redistribution is strictly prohibited. All rights reserved.

prequalification forums, instructions to bidders, information available to bidders, and bid forms. The supplements to bid forms include a bid security form, subcontractor list, and substitution list. The contract forms include the agreement (the contract between the owner and a contractor), performance bond, labor and materials payment bond, and certificates of insurance.

A project manual may contain the following types of specifications:
- Proprietary specifications: Declares that the products made by a particular manufacturer must be used in a project.
- Base-bid specifications (also known as approved equal specifications): Allows public bidding, but declares that a particular proprietary material must be used.
- Descriptive specifications: A type of performance specification in which detailed written requirements for the material or product are given, as well as the workmanship required for its fabrication and installation. Should not mention trade names.
- Reference standard specifications: Outlines the requirements for a proposed design project according to the standards of ANSI, ASTM, or some other acknowledged authority.
- Performance specifications: Indicates the necessary characteristics of the final construction assembly. Does not necessarily indicate how those characteristics will be obtained.
- Pure performance specifications: A type of performance specification which sets the criteria and results required of the item being specified. Results can be verified by measurements, tests, or other types of evaluation. Means of achieving the required results are not specified in the document. These are rarely used because the specifier must know all the criteria and the methods of testing compliance in order to compose an unambiguous document.
- Master specifications: Used by a design office when writing specifications to promote consistency and accuracy. These are prewritten specifications that cover almost all types of products, methods of installation, and any other variables that relate to specific product or construction activity.
- Guide specifications: Similar to master specifications, these are composed to assist the specification writer in the organization of information. Guide specifications indicate the decisions that need to be made and the information that needs to be included in the specification documents.

Technical sections of construction drawings

There is a standard organization for the technical sections of construction drawings. The Construction Specifications Institute and Construction Specifications Canada have developed the Master Format system to standardize the composition of specification documents. It is based on 16 general divisions representing the major categories of work. Part I includes the general requirements for the section, the scope of this section, the submittals required, the warranties, the project conditions,

- 76 -

Copyright © Mometrix Media. You have been licensed one copy of this document for personal use only. Any other reproduction or redistribution is strictly prohibited. All rights reserved.

the delivery specifications, and a protocol for storing and handling materials. Part II includes the specifications for the materials and products (including approved manufacturers), as well as the standards and test methods to which materials must conform and how they must be fabricated. Part III describes how the products and materials are supposed to be installed or applied. This part also will include the examination and preparation required before installation, the quality control protocols, and the requirements for maintaining finished work.

Master format system

Interior designers need to be familiar with the contents of the following divisions in the Master Format system:

- Division 00, procurement and contracting requirements: Includes all of the issues related to bidding and contracting.
- Division 01, general requirements: All of the topics which apply to all of the subsequent individual sections, as well as all general topics which apply to an interior design project.
- Division 02, existing conditions: Includes issues related to site decontamination, remediation, investigation, and demolition.
- Division 03, concrete: Includes forms, reinforcement, precast concrete, cast-in-place concrete, grout, concrete restoration, and concrete cleaning.
- Division 04, masonry: Consideration of brick, stone, terra cotta, glass block, and concrete block, including restoration and cleaning.
- Division 05, metals: Consideration of all structured metals, ornamental metals, and metal fabrications, including restoration and cleaning.
- Division 06, wood, plastics, and composites: Issues related to framing, carpentry, woodwork, restoration, and cleaning.
- Division 07, thermal and moisture protection: Consideration of moisture resistance, air barriers, fire and smoke protection, and roofing supplies that influence heat and water retention.
- Division 08, openings: Discussion of doors, windows, skylights, storefronts, curtains, and glazing.
- Division 09, finishes: Consideration of plaster, gypsum, wallboard, floor tile, wall tile, terrazzo, acoustical ceilings, and any other kind of decorative ceiling or wall covering.
- Division 10, specialties: Includes interior signage, grilles, toilet compartments, lockers, awnings, and flagpoles.
- Division 11, equipment: Consideration of vaults, vending machines, audio-visual equipment, library resources, musical instruments, medical equipment, and any other specialized equipment required for a given space.
- Division 12, furnishings: Includes furniture, systems furniture, window treatments, accessories, and indoor plants.
- Division 13, special construction: Includes seismic control apparatus, rooms supported by air, lightning protection, hot tubs, kennels, and planetariums.

Copyright © Mometrix Media. You have been licensed one copy of this document for personal use only. Any other reproduction or redistribution is strictly prohibited. All rights reserved.

- Division 14, conveying equipment: Consideration of elevators, escalators, lifts, and dumbwaiters.
- Division 21, fire suppression: Consideration of fire detection devices, alarms, and all sorts of fire-extinguishing systems, including foam, carbon dioxide, hoses, and dry-action.
- Division 22, plumbing: Includes all plumbing topics except those related to processing piping, which are covered in the Process Equipment subgroup.
- Division 23, heating, ventilating and air conditioning: Consideration of all topics related to HVAC.
- Division 25, integrated automation: Consideration of energy control, lighting, and other environmental controls.
- Division 26, electrical: Does not include electrical audio, video, and communication equipment.
- Division 27, communications: Consideration of cable, telephone, internet, and speaker systems.
- Division 28, electronic safety and security: Consideration of intrusion detection systems and video surveillance systems.

Contract specification requirements

There are specific requirements that need to be followed in the composition of contract specifications. Specifications are legal documents, so they must be complete, accurate, and clear. The author should know what standards and test methods are included and what parts of them are applicable to a specific project. The author should not conjoin the results and methods proposed to achieve those results. The author should also not include standards that cannot be verified. The author should not put all responsibility on the contractor and should avoid vague or ambiguous language. Each paragraph of a specification document should include only one major idea.

It is important that specifications be aligned closely with the existing construction drawings. Specifications must include all the requirements for materials and construction that the drawings indicated. Construction drawings and technical specifications should use the same terminology. The dimensions and thicknesses should be indicated on only one of the documents. Any notes made on the drawings should not indicate the method of installation or qualities of the material, because this information will be listed in the specifications. Still, the requirements indicated in the construction drawings should not be contradicted by the more detailed information provided in the specifications.

Copyright © Mometrix Media. You have been licensed one copy of this document for personal use only. Any other reproduction or redistribution is strictly prohibited. All rights reserved.

Furniture standards

ANSI has adopted the furniture standards developed by the Business and Institutional Furniture Manufacturers Association, including the following:
- ANSI/BIFMA X5.1, American National Standard for Office Furnishings— General Purpose Office Chairs: Includes criteria for swivel and tilt functions, seating impact, durability, and stability.
- ANSI/BIFMA X5.2, American National Standard for Office Furnishings— Lateral Files: Includes criteria for safety, durability, and structural adequacy.
- ANSI/BIFMA X5.3, American National Standard for Office Furnishings— Vertical Files: Includes criteria for unit stability, lock mechanisms, case racking, drawer cycles, unit strength, and interlock system.
- ANSI/BIFMA X5.4, American National Standard for Office Furnishings— Lounge Seating: Includes criteria for function and safety.
- ANSI/BIFMA X5.5, American National Standard for Office Furnishings—Desk Products: Includes criteria for tipping, stability and durability.
- ANSI/BIFMA X5.6, American National Standard for Office Furnishings—Panel Systems: Includes safety and durability criteria for cubicle walls and other modular partitioning systems.
- ANSI/BIFMA X5.9, American National Standard for Office Furnishings— Storage Units: Includes criteria for safety, durability, and function.
- ANSI/BIFMA S6.5, American National Standard for Office Furnishings—Small Office/Home Office: Includes criteria for safety and function.
- BIFMA G1, Ergonomics Guideline for Visual Display Terminal Furniture Used in Office Work Spaces: Includes criteria for display features and ergonomics.

Furniture specifications

There is an existing set of furniture specifications which interior designers may be called upon to use. This set of specifications is distinct from the Master Format treatment of furnishings in Division 12. Different furniture specifications are used on small, medium, and large-scale commercial projects. In very small-scale projects, the designer may independently purchase and install the furniture, in which case specifications may not be necessary. In some larger residential projects, an interior designer may select the furniture but have the client work directly with the dealer on delivery and installation. In a large-scale project, the designer and client want to solicit bids from multiple dealers for items and accessories.

Contract administration

When an owner holds onto part of each payment made to a contractor in order to protect against poor work, this percentage is called the retainage. Retainage is usually 10%. The date of commencement is the date on which construction is agreed to have begun and therefore, the time from which construction completion time is measured. Substantial completion is the stage and the progress of the work at which

- 79 -

Copyright © Mometrix Media. You have been licensed one copy of this document for personal use only. Any other reproduction or redistribution is strictly prohibited. All rights reserved.

point the work, or a designated portion, is sufficiently complete according to the contract documents that the owner can occupy or utilize this site. A work can be substantially complete even when a few minor items are left to be done or corrected. The contract sum indicates the compensation the contractor will receive for doing the agreed-upon work.

Cost control

During bidding, the following five variables are most likely to affect the cost of the project: project schedule, real cost to the contractor and subcontractors, competitiveness of the market, the contractor's interest in the job, and the profit level desired by the contractor. If a project is predicted to take a very short time or the market is extremely competitive, the bids will be relatively low. Sometimes a contractor will offer a unit price, which is a set cost for providing some of the construction work per unit (for instance, price per square meter).

Copyright © Mometrix Media. You have been licensed one copy of this document for personal use only. Any other reproduction or redistribution is strictly prohibited. All rights reserved.

Contract Administration Process

Contract administration basics

Interior designers need to be familiar with the basics of contract administration. Contract administration is everything done by the designer to facilitate the fulfillment of the contract between owner and contractor. The specific responsibilities of the interior designer during this period are defined in the general conditions of the contract for furniture, furnishings, and equipment. The provisions in this document cover the following topics: submittals, including shop drawings, samples, and product data; field administration, including construction observation, rejection of work, safety, field tests, documentation, claims, mediation, and arbitration; changes in the work, including minor changes in the work, construction change directives, and change orders; progress payments; and installation.

Basic bidding procedures

There is a basic protocol for bidding on construction contracts. Building owners usually alert prospective contractors to an upcoming project by advertising for bids in local newspapers or trade journals or by sending Invitation to Bid forms to possible bidders. In some cases, contractors must pre-qualify before being allowed to bid on the project. This is done when the owner wants to limit bids to those contractors who meet certain standards of reliability, experience, financial stability, and performance. In a negotiated contract, the owner of the building picks a contractor and negotiates with him or her the terms of the contract. In a bid (or tendered) contract, a number of contractors examine contract documents and submit bids. Competitive bidding usually results in the lowest costs for the owner.

Performance bonds

In especially large projects, it may be necessary to include a performance bond. A performance bond is a statement made by a surety company promising that the company will complete construction of the project if the contractor does not. The surety company may complete the construction by hiring another contractor or it may simply give more money to the defaulted contractors so that the construction can proceed. These bonds are usually mandatory on public work. Ultimately, the price will be paid by the owner, because the performance bond is included in the total amount of the contract price.

Labor and material bonds

On large projects, it may be necessary for an owner to procure a labor and material payment bond. A labor and material payment bond guarantees payment for labor and materials for a project in the event that the contractor defaults or does not

Copyright © Mometrix Media. You have been licensed one copy of this document for personal use only. Any other reproduction or redistribution is strictly prohibited. All rights reserved.

make the payments. A performance bond does not make this kind of guarantee. A labor and material payment bond is usually required along with a performance bond, so that the owner is protected against all types of problems. The cost of the labor and material bond is included in the total amount of the contract price.

Copyright © Mometrix Media. You have been licensed one copy of this document for personal use only. Any other reproduction or redistribution is strictly prohibited. All rights reserved.

Finishes, Furnishings, Fixtures, & Equipment

Carpet

Interior designers should be familiar with the following methods of carpet manufacture:
- Weaving: The process of making a carpet on a loom. Backing threads and pile are woven at the same time. Capable of producing complex patterns.
- Wilton: Woven cut, looped, or cut and looped pile. Capable of producing a complicated pattern with a variety of surface textures, although most Wilton carpets are plain.
- Axminster: A woven cut pile carpet which can be short or long and can be woven into an ornate pattern.
- Velvet: Made by a weaving technique in which all the pile yarn is placed on the face of the carpet.
- Tufting: A process in which many needles are used to thread the yarn through the backing at a length of the manufacturer's choice.
- Needle punching: A number of needles are used to wind the fibers through the backing. Can be performed with nylon, jute, or polypropylene. This technique produces a carpet without a pile.
- Fusion bonding: A process of carpet manufacture in which pile tufts are glued directly to the carpet backing.

Interior designers need to be familiar with the accessories and supplementary products used with carpet. Carpet may be attached to the floor or not attached, in which case it is referred to as a rug. Carpet may come in sheet form (that is, in a long roll) or in individual tiles, which are then attached to the floor. Carpets are often accompanied by backing, which lies between the carpet and the floor and provides additional durability and strength to the carpet fiber. Carpet cushions are used to add strength, support the pile yarn, increase dimensional stability, and cushion the foot. Carpet cushions are made of sponge rubber, felt, urethane, and foam rubber.

Tile

Tile is one of the more durable and easy-to-clean surfaces available for finishing. The two common types of tile are ceramic and quarry, although there are some subcategories based on size and method of production.
- Ceramic: A thin tile made out of clay or a clay-based mixture. Can be glazed or unglazed.
- Quarry: Typically larger than ceramic tile. Can be glazed or unglazed. Any non-mosaic tile created through the extrusion method (tiles are cut by machine out of a large clay deposit) is generally referred to as quarry tile.

Copyright © Mometrix Media. You have been licensed one copy of this document for personal use only. Any other reproduction or redistribution is strictly prohibited. All rights reserved.

- Ceramic mosaic: Smaller than quarry tile. Any mosaic tile larger than 6 square inches is classified as wall tile.
- Paver: Any tile larger than 6 square inches created through the dust-pressed method (tiles are pressed out of dry clay).

Tile manufacturers classify tile according to its tendency to absorb water. Water absorption rate is expressed as the percentage of water absorbed when a given amount of water comes into contact with the test material. Tile tends to be more resistant to water when it is glazed and when it has been baked at a higher temperature.
- Non-vitreous: Water absorption rate of more than 7%.
- Semi-vitreous: Water absorption rate of more than 3%, but not more than 7%.
- Vitreous: Water absorption rate of more than 0.5%, but not more than 3%.
- Impervious: Water absorption rate of 0.5% or less.

Flooring tests

Flooring manufacturers subject their products to a number of tests, designed to indicate durability and slip resistance:
- ASTM D2047, Standard Test Method for Static Coefficient of Friction of Polish-Coated Floor Surfaces as Measured by the James Machine: Best measure of slip resistance, although it can only be used on smooth and dry surfaces.
- ASTM C1028, Standard Test Method for Determining the Static Coefficient of Friction of Ceramic Tile and other Like Surfaces by the Horizontal Dynamometer Pull-Meter Method: Less accurate than the James machine, but can be performed on wet, dry, smooth, or rough surfaces. The results of this test can only be compared with results involving the same type of flooring.
- ASTM F1679, Standard Test Method for Using a Variable Incidence Tribometer: Can be performed in any environment and is especially appropriate for dealing with greasy or oily surfaces.
- ASTM F1677, Standard Test Method for Using a Portable Inclinable Articulated Strut Strip Tester: Can be performed in any environment and is especially useful in measuring the effects of grease or oil on slip resistance.
- ASTM F609, Standard Test Method for Using a Horizontal Pull Slipmeter: Assesses the coefficient of friction on the heel of various shoes in contact with flooring.
- ASTM F462, Consumer Safety Specification for Slip-resistant Bathing Facilities: Performed to assess the coefficient of friction on wet and soapy surfaces likely to be found in bathrooms.

Copyright © Mometrix Media. You have been licensed one copy of this document for personal use only. Any other reproduction or redistribution is strictly prohibited. All rights reserved.

Function criteria

When evaluating materials and finishes, interior designers must attend to the following function criteria:
- Acoustic qualities: The ability of a material to absorb sound. Typically measured with the noise reduction coefficient and generally considered to be the most important criteria for finish materials.
- Aesthetics: The appearance of the material or finish.
- Availability of materials: The ease with which a material or finish can be acquired.
- Choices: The amount of variability in color and texture that is available to the designer.
- Installation method: The manner in which the material or finish is applied or implemented. Some methods are more complicated and expensive than others.

Durability criteria

When evaluating materials and finishes, interior designers must attend to the following durability criteria:
- Abrasion resistance: The degree to which a material retains its original surface when rubbed against another object.
- Attachment: The way different materials are connected to one another. It is impossible to attach certain materials to one another.
- Blocking resistance: The degree to which a material resists adhering between the two surfaces of wall covering.
- Breaking strength: The amount of weight required to break a plane of the material. This criterion is typically applied to tile and stone.
- Chemical resistance: The ability of a material or finish to remain undamaged despite exposure to chemicals. Damage includes stains, erosion, breakage, and even subtle changes in appearance or composition.
- Coating adhesion: The ability of a paint or wall covering to adhere to a surface in a thin coat.
- Cold-cracking: The ability of a material surface or finish to maintain its integrity despite low temperatures.
- Colorfastness: The ability of a material surface or finish to retain its color despite exposure to sunlight.
- Corrosion resistance: The ability of a product to avoid being damaged by chemical or electrochemical exposure, especially after exposure to moisture.
- Crocking resistance: The ability of a color to resist transferring its color when rubbed against something else.
- Fabrication quality: The quality of assembly of a product or material. This is especially important when dealing with woodwork.
- Heat-aging resistance: The ability of a wall covering to resist damage due to extended periods of above-average heat.

Copyright © Mometrix Media. You have been licensed one copy of this document for personal use only. Any other reproduction or redistribution is strictly prohibited. All rights reserved.

- Light fastness: The ability of a wall covering, especially paint, to maintain its color despite exposure to sunlight.
- Scrubability: The ability of a material to retain its color and integrity despite being frequently cleaned with soap, water, and detergent.
- Shrinkage: The degree to which a material diminishes in size when it is subjected to moisture.
- Stain resistance: The ability of a material to resist changing its appearance when some other material has been applied and removed.
- Strength/structure: The ability of a material to maintain its integrity and shape when a heavy load is placed on it or when a heavy wind blows against it.
- Tear resistance: The ability of a fabric to keep from tearing further when a small tear already exists.
- Washability: The ability of a material or finish to maintain its normal surface and color qualities when washed frequently with soap, water, and detergent.

Maintainability criteria

When evaluating materials and finishes, interior designers must attend to the following maintainability criteria:
- Cleanability: The ability of the material or finish to be cleaned easily. For instance, a carpet needs to be short enough that it can be vacuumed regularly and easily. This process should not be a distraction for the people that are using the space nor should the cleaning cost be exorbitant.
- Repairability: The ease with which a material or finish can be repaired when it suffers damage or destruction. Small components that are difficult to obtain or assemble will diminish the repairability assessment.
- Resilience: The ability of a material to regain its original shape and structure after it has been bent or smashed by a load of some kind. For instance, a floor pad needs to be able to regain its original shape after someone has walked on it.
- Self-healing quality: Like resilience, this is the ability of a material to regain its former structure after deformation by a load. Whereas resilience is typically applied only to floor surfaces and wall coverings, self-healing quality can be applied to anything.
- Sustainability: The degree to which a product is efficient in its use of resources, both in its creation and use.

Safety and health criteria

When evaluating materials and finishes, interior designers must attend to the following safety and health criteria:
- Mold and mildew resistance: The degree to which a material or finish opposes the growth of microorganisms. Materials should not contain any fibers or chemicals which can be used as food by mold or mildew.

Copyright © Mometrix Media. You have been licensed one copy of this document for personal use only. Any other reproduction or redistribution is strictly prohibited. All rights reserved.

- Finish safety: The surfaces and the edges of the material or finish must not be sharp or protruding in such a way that they can be dangerous to the occupants of a space.
- Flammability: The combustibility of a given material or finish. Includes consideration of the speed with which flame will spread and the amount of smoke that is generated when the material is exposed to fire.
- Outgassing: The release of toxic gasses by a material subsequent to installation. Some of the most common problem gasses are formaldehyde and chlorofluorocarbons.
- Security: The degree to which a product resists theft or damage. This is a particularly important consideration in regards to doors and glazing.
- Slip resistance: In order to measure the slip resistance of a material used in flooring, interior designers will determine the coefficient of friction.
- Volatile organic compound emissions: The degree to which the carbon and hydrogen components of the material will turn into a vapor when exposed to light and air at a normal temperature.

Paint

There is more to paint than color, and interior designers need to know which sort of paint will be appropriate for which sort of job. The two general classifications of paint are water-based and solvent-based. The liquid component of paint is called the vehicle. It is made up of a solvent, which is volatile, and a binder, which is not volatile. The solvent converts the binder into a form that can be applied. The solvent subsequently dries out or evaporates once the paint has been applied. Paint that is used indoors is most susceptible to volatile organic compounds. The most common types of paint are oil, latex, epoxy, and urethane. Oil paint is not used very much these days, because it is sticky and more difficult to apply. Latex paint is the most popular kind of paint at present. Both epoxy and urethane paints supply an extremely durable surface.

Wallpaper and wall coverings

Although wallpaper is used less frequently at present, interior designers still need to be familiar with the basic concepts and techniques related to it. A drop match is a type of wallpaper installation in which pieces are placed next to one another so that the wallpaper pattern is not interrupted. Interior designers may also recommend straight matching, in which strips are aligned horizontally. Other wall coverings include vinyl, fabric, and fiberglass. The three grades of vinyl wall covering are light duty (Type I), medium duty (Type II), and heavy duty (Type III). Fabric wall covering is usually installed in one of the following ways: direct application with an adhesive, in custom-sized fabric panels, with acoustic panels, or with a proprietary stretch wall system. Hydrophobic fabric wall coverings do not absorb or retain moisture. Tackable acoustic fiberglass is a hard board with a hard fiberglass mesh finish. It is composed of a noncombustible fibrous glass mat and a resinous binder.

Copyright © Mometrix Media. You have been licensed one copy of this document for personal use only. Any other reproduction or redistribution is strictly prohibited. All rights reserved.

Sound

There are a few basic physical properties of sound that an interior designer needs to understand before designing an acoustic system. The fundamental qualities of sound are velocity, frequency and power. The velocity of sound is the speed with which it can travel through a given medium. The frequency of sound affects its pitch; higher-pitched sounds have a higher frequency. Frequency is measured in hertz (Hz), which are equal to one sound wave per second. Young people with good hearing can hear a range from 20 Hz to 20,000 Hz. Power is basically the same as loudness. On a logarithmic scale, sound intensity (loudness) is measured in decibels (dB). If a sound increases by 10 dB, a person perceives that the sound has become twice as loud.

Sound transmission

An interior designer needs to understand the various factors that influence the transmission of sound before he or she can design an effective audio and acoustic program for a project. Mass and stiffness are the variables that have the greatest effect on the transmission of sound through a building element. Objects with great mass tend to absorb more sound, while objects with a great deal of stiffness do not absorb sound nearly as well as softer objects. The single-number rating of the ability of an object to dampen the transmission of sound is known as the sound transmission class (STC) of the object.

Sound absorption

An interior designer needs to be aware of the ways that sound can be absorbed, so that he or she can construct an effective acoustic program. Sound absorption is a factor of ceiling materials, flooring, partitions, furniture, and equipment. It is typically measured with the coefficient of absorption, the ratio of sound intensity absorbed by a material to the total amount of sound intensity that reaches the material. The noise reduction coefficient (NRC) is the single-number average of the coefficients of absorption of a given material at 250 Hz, 500 Hz, 1000 Hz, and 2000 Hz. This average is rounded to the nearest 0.05. Reverberation time is the interval required for the sound level in a space to drop by 60 dB after the sound source has stopped production.

Sound control

There are a few common strategies for sound control which an interior designer should be able to identify and prescribe: increasing the mass of the partition, insulating the cavity, sealing any cracks between construction components, adding resilience, and adding sealed openings. The most effective location for sound-absorbing material in a large room is the ceiling. Ceiling attenuation class is the single-number measure of the transmission loss through ceiling tiles between two

Copyright © Mometrix Media. You have been licensed one copy of this document for personal use only. Any other reproduction or redistribution is strictly prohibited. All rights reserved.

closed rooms if there is no barrier above the suspended ceiling. Designers measure speech privacy in open offices with the articulation class and the articulation index. Articulation class indicates how well a ceiling absorbs sound coming over a wall. Articulation index measures the total efficacy of the fully-furnished space.

Copyright © Mometrix Media. You have been licensed one copy of this document for personal use only. Any other reproduction or redistribution is strictly prohibited. All rights reserved.

Environmental

Life-cycle assessment

In order to develop a comprehensive idea about the environmental impact of a material, an interior designer needs to perform a life-cycle assessment. This includes attention to the four main stages of a material's life cycle: acquisition, manufacturing, use/maintenance, and disposal. The interior designer will want to examine how the raw materials for the product are obtained. He or she will also want to determine how the product is assembled, packaged, and delivered. He or she will want to consider the installation, use, and maintenance of the product. Finally, he or she will want to consider what is likely to happen to the product after its period of usefulness has come to an end.

Evaluating building materials

Increasingly, interior designers are being asked to use sustainable building materials. Criteria for the assessment of building materials include the following:

- Embodied energy: The amount of energy it takes to extract, process, and manufacture a product or material.
- Renewable materials: It is better to use materials that can be naturally generated in a short period of time.
- Recycled content: A material is considered more sustainable the more recycled content it contains.
- Energy efficiency: Whenever possible, building materials should diminish the amount of energy required in a building.
- Use of local materials: Reduces transportation expenses and the consumption of fossil fuels.
- Durability: Entails higher initial cost but lower cost over the entire life-cycle.
- Low volatile organic compound content: This criterion is particularly important with the use of adhesives, coatings, and finishes. A building can earn LEED credits for reducing the VOC content.
- Low toxicity: The worst gases emitted by design elements are formaldehyde and chlorofluorocarbons.
- Moisture problems: Materials that tend to become moist can become infected with biological contaminants and unhealthy fungi.
- Water conservation: As much as possible, an interior designer wants to select products that minimize the use of water.
- Maintainability: Specifically, the degree to which a material can be effectively cleaned and maintained with nontoxic chemicals and cleaning supplies.

Copyright © Mometrix Media. You have been licensed one copy of this document for personal use only. Any other reproduction or redistribution is strictly prohibited. All rights reserved.

- Potential for reuse and recycling: Whenever possible designers should opt for materials that can be used again. Products are considered reusable and recyclable even when they have to be converted into a different shape or format.

Salvaged materials

For reasons of sustainability and positive environmental impact, interior designers should strive to use salvaged materials whenever they can. Many interior designers mistakenly believe that it is more expensive to use salvaged materials, but in fact these materials can be quite cheap, especially when the designer cultivates relationships with local junkyards and salvaged material dealers. In particular, designers should be on the lookout for salvaged steel, aluminum, and copper. Aluminum is easily recycled, but uses a lot of energy during manufacture. All of these materials can be reused with excellent results, so long as they have not been covered with damaging chemical compounds.

Wood and plastics

Increasingly, interior designers are discovering the benefits of reusing wood and plastics. There are a few different kinds of wood products that can be incorporated. The simplest is reclaimed wood, which is high-quality lumber salvaged from old construction projects. Interior designers can also explore the world of alternatives to wood, which include particle board and compressed veneer products. Composite wood veneer is made by cutting young, fast-growing trees into veneers, which are then dyed and glued into an artificial log. This log is then sliced again to create the final veneers. Finally, interior designers may want to exclusively use wood products that come from sustainable forests. As for plastics, interior designers should be sure to select plastic products that are recyclable, preferably those derived from previously used plastic materials.

Sustainable finishes

Interior design and finishes are one of the most notorious polluters. Designers are increasingly required to select environmentally conscious chemicals and coatings for their projects. In terms of flooring, designers are increasingly drawn to carpeting made of short nylon fiber, vinyl flooring, or rubber flooring. The best adhesives at present are those based on water and those which use plant resins, primarily. In terms of wall finish, gypsum wall board can be purchased in a 100% recyclable format. Finally, there are a number of acoustical ceiling tiles made entirely out of recycled material.

Sustainable furnishings

More and more, furnishing manufacturers are developing products which are sustainable and which make a positive impact on the environment. This is especially

Copyright © Mometrix Media. You have been licensed one copy of this document for personal use only. Any other reproduction or redistribution is strictly prohibited. All rights reserved.

important because many of the furnishings of the past had hazardous coatings and were made of unsustainable materials. In order to make their projects as green as possible, designers should try to select furnishings made out of recyclable materials and covered with upholstery that is free of formaldehyde. All the fabrics should be biodegradable and colored with nontoxic chemical dyes. Finally, whenever possible, interior designers can reuse or refurbish older furnishings.

Indoor air quality

Interior designers need to be conscious of the ways in which their plans will influence indoor air quality. They need to be aware of the risk of both chemical and biological contaminants. The most common chemical contaminants are known as volatile organic compounds. These substances are found in a number of household products. The EPA is currently developing strict programs for limiting the use of these substances. Formaldehyde is another common chemical contaminant. It is often found in interior adhesives. Biological contaminants include mold, mildew, and fungi. These contaminants typically need moisture in order to grow.

Interior designers need to be familiar with the basic indoor air quality standards. Perhaps the most important piece of legislation on this subject is the Clean Air Act of 1970. This law empowered the Environmental Protection Agency to establish and update standards for indoor air quality. A couple of the more common, voluntary industry standards are ASHRAE Standard 62-2001 and ASHRAE Standard 62.2-2003, which have to do with ventilation and low-rise residential buildings, respectively. The Greenguard Institute has also established a set of rigorous tests for interior design product emissions. These tests supplement the traditional assessments, which include ASTM D5116, ASTM D6670, and ASTM E1333.

Biological contaminants

The nine common biological contaminants found in buildings are mold, mildew, bacteria, viruses, mites, pollen, animal dander, dust, and insects. Mold and mildew both thrive in moist, cool and dark areas, i.e., basements. Bacteria can develop anywhere and can cause infection. Viruses are transmitted by animals, including insects. Mites and insects both can thrive inside partitions and beneath flooring. They are known carriers of disease. Animal dander is an allergen for many people and increases the amount of dust in a space. Pollen is a powderlike substance produced by plants. Finally, dust is mainly composed of human skin and tends to accumulate in high-traffic areas.

Copyright © Mometrix Media. You have been licensed one copy of this document for personal use only. Any other reproduction or redistribution is strictly prohibited. All rights reserved.

Hazardous materials

There are five common hazardous materials found in buildings:
- Asbestos: Often found in older insulation, flooring, caulking, and paint. The inhalation of asbestos fiber often leads to pulmonary fibrosis.
- Vermiculite: Often used as insulation or in potting soil. Often contains asbestos, which can be very dangerous when inhaled.
- Lead: Often found in older kinds of paint. Consumption can lead to brain damage, growth disorders, and death.
- Radon: Not found in building materials, but in surrounding water, rock, and soil. A known cause of cancer, especially when inhaled.
- Polychlorinated biphenyls (PCB): Found in older plastics and rubbers, fluorescent lighting tubes, and paints. Can accumulate in human and animal tissue, resulting in cancer and other health problems.

Recycling and reuse

There are a number of ways for interior designers to incorporate recycling and reuse into their work. Adaptive reuse is the process of using existing buildings and materials rather than creating new ones. Post-industrial materials, also known as pre-consumer materials, are any scrap or trim materials created during the manufacturing process that have been recovered or diverted from solid waste. Post-consumer materials are any materials or products that have served their original purpose but have been recovered from waste. In some cases, it will be impossible to recycle or reuse materials or even buildings. In these cases, interior designers should cooperate with disposal technicians to find environmentally responsible methods of removal and destruction.

Sustainability

There are a few important regulations and industry standards related to sustainability with which all interior designers should be familiar. ASHRAE Standard 90.1 describes the energy efficiency standards for all buildings except low-rise residential units. Standards for product life cycle, building sustainability, and product sustainability are established by ASTM E1991, E2114, and E2129, respectively. The Green Seal organization has established specific standards for paint and windows. Finally, the Toxic Substances Control Act of 1976 empowers the EPA to keep track of all of the chemicals used in household products.

Copyright © Mometrix Media. You have been licensed one copy of this document for personal use only. Any other reproduction or redistribution is strictly prohibited. All rights reserved.

Secret Key #1 - Time is Your Greatest Enemy

Pace Yourself

Wear a watch. At the beginning of the test, check the time (or start a chronometer on your watch to count the minutes), and check the time after every few questions to make sure you are "on schedule."

If you are forced to speed up, do it efficiently. Usually one or more answer choices can be eliminated without too much difficulty. Above all, don't panic. Don't speed up and just begin guessing at random choices. By pacing yourself, and continually monitoring your progress against your watch, you will always know exactly how far ahead or behind you are with your available time. If you find that you are one minute behind on the test, don't skip one question without spending any time on it, just to catch back up. Take 15 fewer seconds on the next four questions, and after four questions you'll have caught back up. Once you catch back up, you can continue working each problem at your normal pace.

Furthermore, don't dwell on the problems that you were rushed on. If a problem was taking up too much time and you made a hurried guess, it must be difficult. The difficult questions are the ones you are most likely to miss anyway, so it isn't a big loss. It is better to end with more time than you need than to run out of time.

Lastly, sometimes it is beneficial to slow down if you are constantly getting ahead of time. You are always more likely to catch a careless mistake by working more slowly than quickly, and among very high-scoring test takers (those who are likely to have lots of time left over), careless errors affect the score more than mastery of material.

Copyright © Mometrix Media. You have been licensed one copy of this document for personal use only. Any other reproduction or redistribution is strictly prohibited. All rights reserved.

Secret Key #2 - Guessing is not Guesswork

You probably know that guessing is a good idea. Unlike other standardized tests, there is no penalty for getting a wrong answer. Even if you have no idea about a question, you still have a 20-25% chance of getting it right.

Most test takers do not understand the impact that proper guessing can have on their score. Unless you score extremely high, guessing will significantly contribute to your final score.

Monkeys Take the Test

What most test takers don't realize is that to insure that 20-25% chance, you have to guess randomly. If you put 20 monkeys in a room to take this test, assuming they answered once per question and behaved themselves, on average they would get 20-25% of the questions correct. Put 20 test takers in the room, and the average will be much lower among guessed questions. Why?

1. The test writers intentionally write deceptive answer choices that "look" right. A test taker has no idea about a question, so he picks the "best looking" answer, which is often wrong. The monkey has no idea what looks good and what doesn't, so it will consistently be right about 20-25% of the time.
2. Test takers will eliminate answer choices from the guessing pool based on a hunch or intuition. Simple but correct answers often get excluded, leaving a 0% chance of being correct. The monkey has no clue, and often gets lucky with the best choice.

This is why the process of elimination endorsed by most test courses is flawed and detrimental to your performance. Test takers don't guess; they make an ignorant stab in the dark that is usually worse than random.

Copyright © Mometrix Media. You have been licensed one copy of this document for personal use only. Any other reproduction or redistribution is strictly prohibited. All rights reserved.

$5 Challenge

Let me introduce one of the most valuable ideas of this course—the $5 challenge:

You only mark your "best guess" if you are willing to bet $5 on it.
You only eliminate choices from guessing if you are willing to bet $5 on it.

Why $5? Five dollars is an amount of money that is small yet not insignificant, and can really add up fast (20 questions could cost you $100). Likewise, each answer choice on one question of the test will have a small impact on your overall score, but it can really add up to a lot of points in the end.

The process of elimination IS valuable. The following shows your chance of guessing it right:

If you eliminate wrong answer choices until only this many remain:	Chance of getting it correct:
1	100%
2	50%
3	33%

However, if you accidentally eliminate the right answer or go on a hunch for an incorrect answer, your chances drop dramatically—to 0%. By guessing among all the answer choices, you are GUARANTEED to have a shot at the right answer.

That's why the $5 test is so valuable. If you give up the advantage and safety of a pure guess, it had better be worth the risk.

What we still haven't covered is how to be sure that whatever guess you make is truly random. Here's the easiest way:

Always pick the first answer choice among those remaining.

Such a technique means that you have decided, **before you see a single test question**, exactly how you are going to guess, and since the order of choices tells you nothing about which one is correct, this guessing technique is perfectly random.

This section is not meant to scare you away from making educated guesses or eliminating choices; you just need to define when a choice is worth eliminating. The $5 test, along with a pre-defined random guessing strategy, is the best way to make sure you reap all of the benefits of guessing.

Copyright © Mometrix Media. You have been licensed one copy of this document for personal use only. Any other reproduction or redistribution is strictly prohibited. All rights reserved.

Secret Key #3 - Practice Smarter, Not Harder

Many test takers delay the test preparation process because they dread the awful amounts of practice time they think necessary to succeed on the test. We have refined an effective method that will take you only a fraction of the time.

There are a number of "obstacles" in the path to success. Among these are answering questions, finishing in time, and mastering test-taking strategies. All must be executed on the day of the test at peak performance, or your score will suffer. The test is a mental marathon that has a large impact on your future.

Just like a marathon runner, it is important to work your way up to the full challenge. So first you just worry about questions, and then time, and finally strategy:

Success Strategy

1. Find a good source for practice tests.
2. If you are willing to make a larger time investment, consider using more than one study guide. Often the different approaches of multiple authors will help you "get" difficult concepts.
3. Take a practice test with no time constraints, with all study helps, "open book." Take your time with questions and focus on applying strategies.
4. Take a practice test with time constraints, with all guides, "open book."
5. Take a final practice test without open material and with time limits.

If you have time to take more practice tests, just repeat step 5. By gradually exposing yourself to the full rigors of the test environment, you will condition your mind to the stress of test day and maximize your success.

Copyright © Mometrix Media. You have been licensed one copy of this document for personal use only. Any other reproduction or redistribution is strictly prohibited. All rights reserved.

Secret Key #4 - Prepare, Don't Procrastinate

Let me state an obvious fact: if you take the test three times, you will probably get three different scores. This is due to the way you feel on test day, the level of preparedness you have, and the version of the test you see. Despite the test writers' claims to the contrary, some versions of the test WILL be easier for you than others.

Since your future depends so much on your score, you should maximize your chances of success. In order to maximize the likelihood of success, you've got to prepare in advance. This means taking practice tests and spending time learning the information and test taking strategies you will need to succeed.

Never go take the actual test as a "practice" test, expecting that you can just take it again if you need to. Take all the practice tests you can on your own, but when you go to take the official test, be prepared, be focused, and do your best the first time!

Copyright © Mometrix Media. You have been licensed one copy of this document for personal use only. Any other reproduction or redistribution is strictly prohibited. All rights reserved.

Secret Key #5 - Test Yourself

Everyone knows that time is money. There is no need to spend too much of your time or too little of your time preparing for the test. You should only spend as much of your precious time preparing as is necessary for you to get the score you need.

Once you have taken a practice test under real conditions of time constraints, then you will know if you are ready for the test or not.

If you have scored extremely high the first time that you take the practice test, then there is not much point in spending countless hours studying. You are already there.

Benchmark your abilities by retaking practice tests and seeing how much you have improved. Once you consistently score high enough to guarantee success, then you are ready.

If you have scored well below where you need, then knuckle down and begin studying in earnest. Check your improvement regularly through the use of practice tests under real conditions. Above all, don't worry, panic, or give up. The key is perseverance!

Then, when you go to take the test, remain confident and remember how well you did on the practice tests. If you can score high enough on a practice test, then you can do the same on the real thing.

Copyright © Mometrix Media. You have been licensed one copy of this document for personal use only. Any other reproduction or redistribution is strictly prohibited. All rights reserved.

General Strategies

The most important thing you can do is to ignore your fears and jump into the test immediately. Do not be overwhelmed by any strange-sounding terms. You have to jump into the test like jumping into a pool—all at once is the easiest way.

Make Predictions

As you read and understand the question, try to guess what the answer will be. Remember that several of the answer choices are wrong, and once you begin reading them, your mind will immediately become cluttered with answer choices designed to throw you off. Your mind is typically the most focused immediately after you have read the question and digested its contents. If you can, try to predict what the correct answer will be. You may be surprised at what you can predict.

Quickly scan the choices and see if your prediction is in the listed answer choices. If it is, then you can be quite confident that you have the right answer. It still won't hurt to check the other answer choices, but most of the time, you've got it!

Answer the Question

It may seem obvious to only pick answer choices that answer the question, but the test writers can create some excellent answer choices that are wrong. Don't pick an answer just because it sounds right, or you believe it to be true. It MUST answer the question. Once you've made your selection, always go back and check it against the question and make sure that you didn't misread the question and that the answer choice does answer the question posed.

Benchmark

After you read the first answer choice, decide if you think it sounds correct or not. If it doesn't, move on to the next answer choice. If it does, mentally mark that answer choice. This doesn't mean that you've definitely selected it as your answer choice, it just means that it's the best you've seen thus far. Go ahead and read the next choice. If the next choice is worse than the one you've already selected, keep going to the next answer choice. If the next choice is better than the choice you've already selected, mentally mark the new answer choice as your best guess.

The first answer choice that you select becomes your standard. Every other answer choice must be benchmarked against that standard. That choice is correct until proven otherwise by another answer choice beating it out. Once you've decided that no other answer choice seems as good, do one final check to ensure that your answer choice answers the question posed.

Valid Information

Don't discount any of the information provided in the question. Every piece of information may be necessary to determine the correct answer. None of the

Copyright © Mometrix Media. You have been licensed one copy of this document for personal use only. Any other reproduction or redistribution is strictly prohibited. All rights reserved.

information in the question is there to throw you off (while the answer choices will certainly have information to throw you off). If two seemingly unrelated topics are discussed, don't ignore either. You can be confident there is a relationship, or it wouldn't be included in the question, and you are probably going to have to determine what is that relationship to find the answer.

Avoid "Fact Traps"

Don't get distracted by a choice that is factually true. Your search is for the answer that answers the question. Stay focused and don't fall for an answer that is true but irrelevant. Always go back to the question and make sure you're choosing an answer that actually answers the question and is not just a true statement. An answer can be factually correct, but it MUST answer the question asked. Additionally, two answers can both be seemingly correct, so be sure to read all of the answer choices, and make sure that you get the one that BEST answers the question.

Milk the Question

Some of the questions may throw you completely off. They might deal with a subject you have not been exposed to, or one that you haven't reviewed in years. While your lack of knowledge about the subject will be a hindrance, the question itself can give you many clues that will help you find the correct answer. Read the question carefully and look for clues. Watch particularly for adjectives and nouns describing difficult terms or words that you don't recognize. Regardless of whether you completely understand a word or not, replacing it with a synonym, either provided or one you more familiar with, may help you to understand what the questions are asking. Rather than wracking your mind about specific detailed information concerning a difficult term or word, try to use mental substitutes that are easier to understand.

The Trap of Familiarity

Don't just choose a word because you recognize it. On difficult questions, you may not recognize a number of words in the answer choices. The test writers don't put "make-believe" words on the test, so don't think that just because you only recognize all the words in one answer choice that that answer choice must be correct. If you only recognize words in one answer choice, then focus on that one. Is it correct? Try your best to determine if it is correct. If it is, that's great. If not, eliminate it. Each word and answer choice you eliminate increases your chances of getting the question correct, even if you then have to guess among the unfamiliar choices.

Eliminate Answers

Eliminate choices as soon as you realize they are wrong. But be careful! Make sure you consider all of the possible answer choices. Just because one appears right, doesn't mean that the next one won't be even better! The test writers will usually put more than one good answer choice for every question, so read all of them. Don't worry if you are stuck between two that seem right. By getting down to just two remaining possible choices, your odds are now 50/50. Rather than wasting too

Copyright © Mometrix Media. You have been licensed one copy of this document for personal use only. Any other reproduction or redistribution is strictly prohibited. All rights reserved.

much time, play the odds. You are guessing, but guessing wisely because you've been able to knock out some of the answer choices that you know are wrong. If you are eliminating choices and realize that the last answer choice you are left with is also obviously wrong, don't panic. Start over and consider each choice again. There may easily be something that you missed the first time and will realize on the second pass.

Tough Questions

If you are stumped on a problem or it appears too hard or too difficult, don't waste time. Move on! Remember though, if you can quickly check for obviously incorrect answer choices, your chances of guessing correctly are greatly improved. Before you completely give up, at least try to knock out a couple of possible answers. Eliminate what you can and then guess at the remaining answer choices before moving on.

Brainstorm

If you get stuck on a difficult question, spend a few seconds quickly brainstorming. Run through the complete list of possible answer choices. Look at each choice and ask yourself, "Could this answer the question satisfactorily?" Go through each answer choice and consider it independently of the others. By systematically going through all possibilities, you may find something that you would otherwise overlook. Remember though that when you get stuck, it's important to try to keep moving.

Read Carefully

Understand the problem. Read the question and answer choices carefully. Don't miss the question because you misread the terms. You have plenty of time to read each question thoroughly and make sure you understand what is being asked. Yet a happy medium must be attained, so don't waste too much time. You must read carefully, but efficiently.

Face Value

When in doubt, use common sense. Always accept the situation in the problem at face value. Don't read too much into it. These problems will not require you to make huge leaps of logic. The test writers aren't trying to throw you off with a cheap trick. If you have to go beyond creativity and make a leap of logic in order to have an answer choice answer the question, then you should look at the other answer choices. Don't overcomplicate the problem by creating theoretical relationships or explanations that will warp time or space. These are normal problems rooted in reality. It's just that the applicable relationship or explanation may not be readily apparent and you have to figure things out. Use your common sense to interpret anything that isn't clear.

Prefixes

If you're having trouble with a word in the question or answer choices, try dissecting it. Take advantage of every clue that the word might include. Prefixes

Copyright © Mometrix Media. You have been licensed one copy of this document for personal use only. Any other reproduction or redistribution is strictly prohibited. All rights reserved.

and suffixes can be a huge help. Usually they allow you to determine a basic meaning. Pre- means before, post- means after, pro - is positive, de- is negative. From these prefixes and suffixes, you can get an idea of the general meaning of the word and try to put it into context. Beware though of any traps. Just because con- is the opposite of pro-, doesn't necessarily mean congress is the opposite of progress!

Hedge Phrases

Watch out for critical hedge phrases, led off with words such as "likely," "may," "can," "sometimes," "often," "almost," "mostly," "usually," "generally," "rarely," and "sometimes." Question writers insert these hedge phrases to cover every possibility. Often an answer choice will be wrong simply because it leaves no room for exception. Unless the situation calls for them, avoid answer choices that have definitive words like "exactly," and "always."

Switchback Words

Stay alert for "switchbacks." These are the words and phrases frequently used to alert you to shifts in thought. The most common switchback word is "but." Others include "although," "however," "nevertheless," "on the other hand," "even though," "while," "in spite of," "despite," and "regardless of."

New Information

Correct answer choices will rarely have completely new information included. Answer choices typically are straightforward reflections of the material asked about and will directly relate to the question. If a new piece of information is included in an answer choice that doesn't even seem to relate to the topic being asked about, then that answer choice is likely incorrect. All of the information needed to answer the question is usually provided for you in the question. You should not have to make guesses that are unsupported or choose answer choices that require unknown information that cannot be reasoned from what is given.

Time Management

On technical questions, don't get lost on the technical terms. Don't spend too much time on any one question. If you don't know what a term means, then odds are you aren't going to get much further since you don't have a dictionary. You should be able to immediately recognize whether or not you know a term. If you don't, work with the other clues that you have—the other answer choices and terms provided— but don't waste too much time trying to figure out a difficult term that you don't know.

Contextual Clues

Look for contextual clues. An answer can be right but not the correct answer. The contextual clues will help you find the answer that is most right and is correct. Understand the context in which a phrase or statement is made. This will help you make important distinctions.

Copyright © Mometrix Media. You have been licensed one copy of this document for personal use only. Any other reproduction or redistribution is strictly prohibited. All rights reserved.

Don't Panic

Panicking will not answer any questions for you; therefore, it isn't helpful. When you first see the question, if your mind goes blank, take a deep breath. Force yourself to mechanically go through the steps of solving the problem using the strategies you've learned.

Pace Yourself

Don't get clock fever. It's easy to be overwhelmed when you're looking at a page full of questions, your mind is full of random thoughts and feeling confused, and the clock is ticking down faster than you would like. Calm down and maintain the pace that you have set for yourself. As long as you are on track by monitoring your pace, you are guaranteed to have enough time for yourself. When you get to the last few minutes of the test, it may seem like you won't have enough time left, but if you only have as many questions as you should have left at that point, then you're right on track!

Answer Selection

The best way to pick an answer choice is to eliminate all of those that are wrong, until only one is left and confirm that is the correct answer. Sometimes though, an answer choice may immediately look right. Be careful! Take a second to make sure that the other choices are not equally obvious. Don't make a hasty mistake. There are only two times that you should stop before checking other answers. First is when you are positive that the answer choice you have selected is correct. Second is when time is almost out and you have to make a quick guess!

Check Your Work

Since you will probably not know every term listed and the answer to every question, it is important that you get credit for the ones that you do know. Don't miss any questions through careless mistakes. If at all possible, try to take a second to look back over your answer selection and make sure you've selected the correct answer choice and haven't made a costly careless mistake (such as marking an answer choice that you didn't mean to mark). The time it takes for this quick double check should more than pay for itself in caught mistakes.

Beware of Directly Quoted Answers

Sometimes an answer choice will repeat word for word a portion of the question or reference section. However, beware of such exact duplication. It may be a trap! More than likely, the correct choice will paraphrase or summarize a point, rather than being exactly the same wording.

Slang

Scientific sounding answers are better than slang ones. An answer choice that begins "To compare the outcomes..." is much more likely to be correct than one that begins "Because some people insisted..."

Copyright © Mometrix Media. You have been licensed one copy of this document for personal use only. Any other reproduction or redistribution is strictly prohibited. All rights reserved.

Extreme Statements

Avoid wild answers that throw out highly controversial ideas that are proclaimed as established fact. An answer choice that states the "process should used in certain situations, if..." is much more likely to be correct than one that states the "process should be discontinued completely." The first is a calm rational statement and doesn't even make a definitive, uncompromising stance, using a hedge word "if" to provide wiggle room, whereas the second choice is a radical idea and far more extreme.

Answer Choice Families

When you have two or more answer choices that are direct opposites or parallels, one of them is usually the correct answer. For instance, if one answer choice states "x increases" and another answer choice states "x decreases" or "y increases," then those two or three answer choices are very similar in construction and fall into the same family of answer choices. A family of answer choices consists of two or three answer choices, very similar in construction, but often with directly opposite meanings. Usually the correct answer choice will be in that family of answer choices. The "odd man out" or answer choice that doesn't seem to fit the parallel construction of the other answer choices is more likely to be incorrect.

Copyright © Mometrix Media. You have been licensed one copy of this document for personal use only. Any other reproduction or redistribution is strictly prohibited. All rights reserved.

Special Report: How to Overcome Test Anxiety

The very nature of tests caters to some level of anxiety, nervousness, or tension, just as we feel for any important event that occurs in our lives. A little bit of anxiety or nervousness can be a good thing. It helps us with motivation, and makes achievement just that much sweeter. However, too much anxiety can be a problem, especially if it hinders our ability to function and perform.

"Test anxiety," is the term that refers to the emotional reactions that some test-takers experience when faced with a test or exam. Having a fear of testing and exams is based upon a rational fear, since the test-taker's performance can shape the course of an academic career. Nevertheless, experiencing excessive fear of examinations will only interfere with the test-taker's ability to perform and chance to be successful.

There are a large variety of causes that can contribute to the development and sensation of test anxiety. These include, but are not limited to, lack of preparation and worrying about issues surrounding the test.

Lack of Preparation

Lack of preparation can be identified by the following behaviors or situations:

Not scheduling enough time to study, and therefore cramming the night before the test or exam
Managing time poorly, to create the sensation that there is not enough time to do everything
Failing to organize the text information in advance, so that the study material consists of the entire text and not simply the pertinent information
Poor overall studying habits

Worrying, on the other hand, can be related to both the test taker, or many other factors around him/her that will be affected by the results of the test. These include worrying about:

Previous performances on similar exams, or exams in general
How friends and other students are achieving
The negative consequences that will result from a poor grade or failure

There are three primary elements to test anxiety. Physical components, which involve the same typical bodily reactions as those to acute anxiety (to be discussed below). Emotional factors have to do with fear or panic. Mental or cognitive issues concerning attention spans and memory abilities.

Copyright © Mometrix Media. You have been licensed one copy of this document for personal use only. Any other reproduction or redistribution is strictly prohibited. All rights reserved.

Physical Signals

There are many different symptoms of test anxiety, and these are not limited to mental and emotional strain. Frequently there are a range of physical signals that will let a test taker know that he/she is suffering from test anxiety. These bodily changes can include the following:

Perspiring
Sweaty palms
Wet, trembling hands
Nausea
Dry mouth
A knot in the stomach
Headache
Faintness
Muscle tension
Aching shoulders, back and neck
Rapid heart beat
Feeling too hot/cold

To recognize the sensation of test anxiety, a test-taker should monitor him/herself for the following sensations:

The physical distress symptoms as listed above
Emotional sensitivity, expressing emotional feelings such as the need to cry or laugh too much, or a sensation of anger or helplessness
A decreased ability to think, causing the test-taker to blank out or have racing thoughts that are hard to organize or control.

Though most students will feel some level of anxiety when faced with a test or exam, the majority can cope with that anxiety and maintain it at a manageable level. However, those who cannot are faced with a very real and very serious condition, which can and should be controlled for the immeasurable benefit of this sufferer.

Naturally, these sensations lead to negative results for the testing experience. The most common effects of test anxiety have to do with nervousness and mental blocking.

Nervousness

Nervousness can appear in several different levels:

The test-taker's difficulty, or even inability to read and understand the questions on the test

Copyright © Mometrix Media. You have been licensed one copy of this document for personal use only. Any other reproduction or redistribution is strictly prohibited. All rights reserved.

The difficulty or inability to organize thoughts to a coherent form
The difficulty or inability to recall key words and concepts relating to the testing questions (especially essays)
The receipt of poor grades on a test, though the test material was well known by the test taker

Conversely, a person may also experience mental blocking, which involves:

Blanking out on test questions
Only remembering the correct answers to the questions when the test has already finished.

Fortunately for test anxiety sufferers, beating these feelings, to a large degree, has to do with proper preparation. When a test taker has a feeling of preparedness, then anxiety will be dramatically lessened.

The first step to resolving anxiety issues is to distinguish which of the two types of anxiety are being suffered. If the anxiety is a direct result of a lack of preparation, this should be considered a normal reaction, and the anxiety level (as opposed to the test results) shouldn't be anything to worry about. However, if, when adequately prepared, the test-taker still panics, blanks out, or seems to overreact, this is not a fully rational reaction. While this can be considered normal too, there are many ways to combat and overcome these effects.

Remember that anxiety cannot be entirely eliminated, however, there are ways to minimize it, to make the anxiety easier to manage. Preparation is one of the best ways to minimize test anxiety. Therefore the following techniques are wise in order to best fight off any anxiety that may want to build.

To begin with, try to avoid cramming before a test, whenever it is possible. By trying to memorize an entire term's worth of information in one day, you'll be shocking your system, and not giving yourself a very good chance to absorb the information. This is an easy path to anxiety, so for those who suffer from test anxiety, cramming should not even be considered an option.

Instead of cramming, work throughout the semester to combine all of the material which is presented throughout the semester, and work on it gradually as the course goes by, making sure to master the main concepts first, leaving minor details for a week or so before the test.

To study for the upcoming exam, be sure to pose questions that may be on the examination, to gauge the ability to answer them by integrating the ideas from your texts, notes and lectures, as well as any supplementary readings.

If it is truly impossible to cover all of the information that was covered in that particular term, concentrate on the most important portions, that can be covered

Copyright © Mometrix Media. You have been licensed one copy of this document for personal use only. Any other reproduction or redistribution is strictly prohibited. All rights reserved.

very well. Learn these concepts as best as possible, so that when the test comes, a goal can be made to use these concepts as presentations of your knowledge.

In addition to study habits, changes in attitude are critical to beating a struggle with test anxiety. In fact, an improvement of the perspective over the entire test-taking experience can actually help a test taker to enjoy studying and therefore improve the overall experience. Be certain not to overemphasize the significance of the grade - know that the result of the test is neither a reflection of self worth, nor is it a measure of intelligence; one grade will not predict a person's future success.

To improve an overall testing outlook, the following steps should be tried:

Keeping in mind that the most reasonable expectation for taking a test is to expect to try to demonstrate as much of what you know as you possibly can. Reminding ourselves that a test is only one test; this is not the only one, and there will be others.
The thought of thinking of oneself in an irrational, all-or-nothing term should be avoided at all costs.
A reward should be designated for after the test, so there's something to look forward to. Whether it be going to a movie, going out to eat, or simply visiting friends, schedule it in advance, and do it no matter what result is expected on the exam.

Test-takers should also keep in mind that the basics are some of the most important things, even beyond anti-anxiety techniques and studying. Never neglect the basic social, emotional and biological needs, in order to try to absorb information. In order to best achieve, these three factors must be held as just as important as the studying itself.

Study Steps

Remember the following important steps for studying:

Maintain healthy nutrition and exercise habits. Continue both your recreational activities and social pass times. These both contribute to your physical and emotional well being.
Be certain to get a good amount of sleep, especially the night before the test, because when you're overtired you are not able to perform to the best of your best ability.
Keep the studying pace to a moderate level by taking breaks when they are needed, and varying the work whenever possible, to keep the mind fresh instead of getting bored.
When enough studying has been done that all the material that can be learned has been learned, and the test taker is prepared for the test, stop studying and do

Copyright © Mometrix Media. You have been licensed one copy of this document for personal use only. Any other reproduction or redistribution is strictly prohibited. All rights reserved.

something relaxing such as listening to music, watching a movie, or taking a warm bubble bath.

There are also many other techniques to minimize the uneasiness or apprehension that is experienced along with test anxiety before, during, or even after the examination. In fact, there are a great deal of things that can be done to stop anxiety from interfering with lifestyle and performance. Again, remember that anxiety will not be eliminated entirely, and it shouldn't be. Otherwise that "up" feeling for exams would not exist, and most of us depend on that sensation to perform better than usual. However, this anxiety has to be at a level that is manageable.

Of course, as we have just discussed, being prepared for the exam is half the battle right away. Attending all classes, finding out what knowledge will be expected on the exam, and knowing the exam schedules are easy steps to lowering anxiety. Keeping up with work will remove the need to cram, and efficient study habits will eliminate wasted time. Studying should be done in an ideal location for concentration, so that it is simple to become interested in the material and give it complete attention. A method such as SQ3R (Survey, Question, Read, Recite, Review) is a wonderful key to follow to make sure that the study habits are as effective as possible, especially in the case of learning from a textbook. Flashcards are great techniques for memorization. Learning to take good notes will mean that notes will be full of useful information, so that less sifting will need to be done to seek out what is pertinent for studying. Reviewing notes after class and then again on occasion will keep the information fresh in the mind. From notes that have been taken summary sheets and outlines can be made for simpler reviewing.

A study group can also be a very motivational and helpful place to study, as there will be a sharing of ideas, all of the minds can work together, to make sure that everyone understands, and the studying will be made more interesting because it will be a social occasion.

Basically, though, as long as the test-taker remains organized and self confident, with efficient study habits, less time will need to be spent studying, and higher grades will be achieved.

To become self confident, there are many useful steps. The first of these is "self talk." It has been shown through extensive research, that self-talk for students who suffer from test anxiety, should be well monitored, in order to make sure that it contributes to self confidence as opposed to sinking the student. Frequently the self talk of test-anxious students is negative or self-defeating, thinking that everyone else is smarter and faster, that they always mess up, and that if they don't do well, they'll fail the entire course. It is important to decreasing anxiety that awareness is made of self talk. Try writing any negative self thoughts and then disputing them with a positive statement instead. Begin

Copyright © Mometrix Media. You have been licensed one copy of this document for personal use only. Any other reproduction or redistribution is strictly prohibited. All rights reserved.

self-encouragement as though it was a friend speaking. Repeat positive statements to help reprogram the mind to believing in successes instead of failures.

Helpful Techniques

Other extremely helpful techniques include:

Self-visualization of doing well and reaching goals
While aiming for an "A" level of understanding, don't try to "overprotect" by setting your expectations lower. This will only convince the mind to stop studying in order to meet the lower expectations.
Don't make comparisons with the results or habits of other students. These are individual factors, and different things work for different people, causing different results.
Strive to become an expert in learning what works well, and what can be done in order to improve. Consider collecting this data in a journal.
Create rewards for after studying instead of doing things before studying that will only turn into avoidance behaviors.
Make a practice of relaxing - by using methods such as progressive relaxation, self-hypnosis, guided imagery, etc - in order to make relaxation an automatic sensation.
Work on creating a state of relaxed concentration so that concentrating will take on the focus of the mind, so that none will be wasted on worrying.
Take good care of the physical self by eating well and getting enough sleep.
Plan in time for exercise and stick to this plan.

Beyond these techniques, there are other methods to be used before, during and after the test that will help the test-taker perform well in addition to overcoming anxiety.

Before the exam comes the academic preparation. This involves establishing a study schedule and beginning at least one week before the actual date of the test. By doing this, the anxiety of not having enough time to study for the test will be automatically eliminated. Moreover, this will make the studying a much more effective experience, ensuring that the learning will be an easier process. This relieves much undue pressure on the test-taker.

Summary sheets, note cards, and flash cards with the main concepts and examples of these main concepts should be prepared in advance of the actual studying time. A topic should never be eliminated from this process. By omitting a topic because it isn't expected to be on the test is only setting up the test-taker for anxiety should it actually appear on the exam. Utilize the course syllabus for laying out the topics that should be studied. Carefully go over the notes that were made in class, paying special attention to any of the issues that

Copyright © Mometrix Media. You have been licensed one copy of this document for personal use only. Any other reproduction or redistribution is strictly prohibited. All rights reserved.

the professor took special care to emphasize while lecturing in class. In the textbooks, use the chapter review, or if possible, the chapter tests, to begin your review.

It may even be possible to ask the instructor what information will be covered on the exam, or what the format of the exam will be (for example, multiple choice, essay, free form, true-false). Additionally, see if it is possible to find out how many questions will be on the test. If a review sheet or sample test has been offered by the professor, make good use of it, above anything else, for the preparation for the test. Another great resource for getting to know the examination is reviewing tests from previous semesters. Use these tests to review, and aim to achieve a 100% score on each of the possible topics. With a few exceptions, the goal that you set for yourself is the highest one that you will reach.

Take all of the questions that were assigned as homework, and rework them to any other possible course material. The more problems reworked, the more skill and confidence will form as a result. When forming the solution to a problem, write out each of the steps. Don't simply do head work. By doing as many steps on paper as possible, much clarification and therefore confidence will be formed. Do this with as many homework problems as possible, before checking the answers. By checking the answer after each problem, a reinforcement will exist, that will not be on the exam. Study situations should be as exam-like as possible, to prime the test-taker's system for the experience. By waiting to check the answers at the end, a psychological advantage will be formed, to decrease the stress factor.

Another fantastic reason for not cramming is the avoidance of confusion in concepts, especially when it comes to mathematics. 8-10 hours of study will become one hundred percent more effective if it is spread out over a week or at least several days, instead of doing it all in one sitting. Recognize that the human brain requires time in order to assimilate new material, so frequent breaks and a span of study time over several days will be much more beneficial.

Additionally, don't study right up until the point of the exam. Studying should stop a minimum of one hour before the exam begins. This allows the brain to rest and put things in their proper order. This will also provide the time to become as relaxed as possible when going into the examination room. The test-taker will also have time to eat well and eat sensibly. Know that the brain needs food as much as the rest of the body. With enough food and enough sleep, as well as a relaxed attitude, the body and the mind are primed for success.

Avoid any anxious classmates who are talking about the exam. These students only spread anxiety, and are not worth sharing the anxious sentimentalities.

Copyright © Mometrix Media. You have been licensed one copy of this document for personal use only. Any other reproduction or redistribution is strictly prohibited. All rights reserved.

Before the test also involves creating a positive attitude, so mental preparation should also be a point of concentration. There are many keys to creating a positive attitude. Should fears become rushing in, make a visualization of taking the exam, doing well, and seeing an A written on the paper. Write out a list of affirmations that will bring a feeling of confidence, such as "I am doing well in my English class," "I studied well and know my material," "I enjoy this class." Even if the affirmations aren't believed at first, it sends a positive message to the subconscious which will result in an alteration of the overall belief system, which is the system that creates reality.

If a sensation of panic begins, work with the fear and imagine the very worst! Work through the entire scenario of not passing the test, failing the entire course, and dropping out of school, followed by not getting a job, and pushing a shopping cart through the dark alley where you'll live. This will place things into perspective! Then, practice deep breathing and create a visualization of the opposite situation - achieving an "A" on the exam, passing the entire course, receiving the degree at a graduation ceremony.

On the day of the test, there are many things to be done to ensure the best results, as well as the most calm outlook. The following stages are suggested in order to maximize test-taking potential:

Begin the examination day with a moderate breakfast, and avoid any coffee or beverages with caffeine if the test taker is prone to jitters. Even people who are used to managing caffeine can feel jittery or light-headed when it is taken on a test day.
Attempt to do something that is relaxing before the examination begins. As last minute cramming clouds the mastering of overall concepts, it is better to use this time to create a calming outlook.
Be certain to arrive at the test location well in advance, in order to provide time to select a location that is away from doors, windows and other distractions, as well as giving enough time to relax before the test begins.
Keep away from anxiety generating classmates who will upset the sensation of stability and relaxation that is being attempted before the exam.
Should the waiting period before the exam begins cause anxiety, create a self-distraction by reading a light magazine or something else that is relaxing and simple.

During the exam itself, read the entire exam from beginning to end, and find out how much time should be allotted to each individual problem. Once writing the exam, should more time be taken for a problem, it should be abandoned, in order to begin another problem. If there is time at the end, the unfinished problem can always be returned to and completed.

Read the instructions very carefully - twice - so that unpleasant surprises won't follow during or after the exam has ended.

Copyright © Mometrix Media. You have been licensed one copy of this document for personal use only. Any other reproduction or redistribution is strictly prohibited. All rights reserved.

When writing the exam, pretend that the situation is actually simply the completion of homework within a library, or at home. This will assist in forming a relaxed atmosphere, and will allow the brain extra focus for the complex thinking function.

Begin the exam with all of the questions with which the most confidence is felt. This will build the confidence level regarding the entire exam and will begin a quality momentum. This will also create encouragement for trying the problems where uncertainty resides.

Going with the "gut instinct" is always the way to go when solving a problem. Second guessing should be avoided at all costs. Have confidence in the ability to do well.

For essay questions, create an outline in advance that will keep the mind organized and make certain that all of the points are remembered. For multiple choice, read every answer, even if the correct one has been spotted - a better one may exist.

Continue at a pace that is reasonable and not rushed, in order to be able to work carefully. Provide enough time to go over the answers at the end, to check for small errors that can be corrected.

Should a feeling of panic begin, breathe deeply, and think of the feeling of the body releasing sand through its pores. Visualize a calm, peaceful place, and include all of the sights, sounds and sensations of this image. Continue the deep breathing, and take a few minutes to continue this with closed eyes. When all is well again, return to the test.

If a "blanking" occurs for a certain question, skip it and move on to the next question. There will be time to return to the other question later. Get everything done that can be done, first, to guarantee all the grades that can be compiled, and to build all of the confidence possible. Then return to the weaker questions to build the marks from there.

Remember, one's own reality can be created, so as long as the belief is there, success will follow. And remember: anxiety can happen later, right now, there's an exam to be written!

After the examination is complete, whether there is a feeling for a good grade or a bad grade, don't dwell on the exam, and be certain to follow through on the reward that was promised...and enjoy it! Don't dwell on any mistakes that have been made, as there is nothing that can be done at this point anyway.

Copyright © Mometrix Media. You have been licensed one copy of this document for personal use only. Any other reproduction or redistribution is strictly prohibited. All rights reserved.

Additionally, don't begin to study for the next test right away. Do something relaxing for a while, and let the mind relax and prepare itself to begin absorbing information again.

From the results of the exam - both the grade and the entire experience, be certain to learn from what has gone on. Perfect studying habits and work some more on confidence in order to make the next examination experience even better than the last one.

Learn to avoid places where openings occurred for laziness, procrastination and day dreaming.

Use the time between this exam and the next one to better learn to relax, even learning to relax on cue, so that any anxiety can be controlled during the next exam. Learn how to relax the body. Slouch in your chair if that helps. Tighten and then relax all of the different muscle groups, one group at a time, beginning with the feet and then working all the way up to the neck and face. This will ultimately relax the muscles more than they were to begin with. Learn how to breathe deeply and comfortably, and focus on this breathing going in and out as a relaxing thought. With every exhale, repeat the word "relax."

As common as test anxiety is, it is very possible to overcome it. Make yourself one of the test-takers who overcome this frustrating hindrance.

Copyright © Mometrix Media. You have been licensed one copy of this document for personal use only. Any other reproduction or redistribution is strictly prohibited. All rights reserved.

Additional Bonus Material

Due to our efforts to try to keep this book to a manageable length, we've created a link that will give you access to all of your additional bonus material.

Please visit http://www.mometrix.com/bonus948/idex to access the information.

Copyright © Mometrix Media. You have been licensed one copy of this document for personal use only. Any other reproduction or redistribution is strictly prohibited. All rights reserved.